RUNNING RIOT

RUNNING RIOT

A Journey Through
the Official Disasters
and Creative Disorder
in American Society

Arthur I. Waskow

An *Azimuth* Book
Herder and Herder

1970
HERDER AND HERDER NEW YORK
232 Madison Avenue, New York 10016

Library of Congress Catalog Card Number: 70–110796
© 1970 by Arthur I. Waskow
Manufactured in the United States

Contents

I have learned much from my teachers,
still more from my colleagues,
but from my students most of all.
—*Pirke Aboth*

For Carol McEldowney, Todd Gitlin,
Jeremy Brecher, Charlotte Bunch-Weeks,
Nancy Bancroft, Judy Coburn, Sue Orrin,
Marc Sommer, Joan Bowman, Mike Grossman,
Paul Booth, Sue Strauss, Frank Smith,
Sue Thrasher, Charles Sherrod, Paul Gorman,
Rick Margolies, John McAuliff, and Greg Finger.

Introduction

Today is Saturday, February 14, 1970, and I am waiting, full of dread, to hear from Chicago what is happening to my friends in "the Conspiracy." The jury is going out this morning, and the judge was overheard the other day to say that he would put the lot of them in jail at once, for contempt. So I may not see Tom Hayden, or Dave Dellinger, or Rennie Davis again for years . . . Which feels very strange, and horrifying, and infuriating.

The movement began almost exactly ten years ago today, with the first sit-ins. I had come to Washington just four months before, to write a Ph.D. dissertation about some long-forgotten race riots—a subject that seemed abstruse and quaint in those days—and to work for a United States Congressman. I thought I was trying to reconstruct liberalism, political and intellectual. And meanwhile people like Tom Hayden were just barely beginning to think about reconstructing radicalism. I didn't even know they existed. Now I can't get my mind off the notion of Tom in jail.

When did I first meet him? I can't remember; but I recall hearing his name as the victim of a police beating in McComb, Mississippi, when I first met the early fragments of the movement in 1962. They were coming to Washington to explain to Mac Bundy about the uselessness of "deterrence." (They thought he might change his mind. They really did.)

It is a strange day to be writing an introduction to a book about change in America—"Amerika," the movement calls it now. The Conspiracy is accused of planning a riot in Chicago. My book is called *Running Riot*. But it's not about them, or about the Blacks who burned down Newark. It's about that Amerika which wants to jail them. *That* is what's running riot.

I could hardly have begun to grasp such an idea in 1959, when I arrived in Washington. It took years of coping with one Amerikan "riot" after another for me to begin to believe they were happening. Some of them involved me in such direct ways as to become especially vivid:

As when I discovered, while doing research on germ warfare for a Congressman, that the Chemical Corps's talk about "humane non-lethal weapons" was a cover for stockpiling the Black Plague . . . and three generals in full regalia came marching into my Congressman's office to tell us to lay off.

As when in October 1962 I spent a desperate back-to-the-wall week in Washington, trying to find ways to stop a "liberal" President from blowing up the world for a marginal military-political gain . . . and spent a long night listening to Leo Szilard say how useless all my efforts were, and advise me and all his callers to fly out of the country.

As in July 1963 when I joined an anti-segregation walk-in and found myself attacked by a racist mob and arrested by the police—who didn't even think of arresting the mob . . . and rode away to jail simultaneously crying and singing "Maryland will be free."

As in March 1965, when I spoke at the first teach-in at Ann Arbor to say that the government's attack on North Vietnam made me remember Jefferson's line, "I tremble for my country when I reflect that God is just" . . . and had my speech stopped by police who said they had received a bomb threat and must clear the hall.

As in . . . a dozen cases more.

It is no new discovery, now, to say that the United States government ran riot throughout the '60s. It was a new discovery every moment when it happened *during* the '60s.

This book is a journey through what I have called the official disasters and creative disorders of this decade. It has been a journey for me, from the days when I felt like a citizen possessed of all the power the civics books said I had—but was in reality a bureaucratized checker of other people's footnotes and myself a footnote to the country's politics—toward a place where I know myself unable to control the great institutions, but precisely from that knowledge begin to reach out to my powerless brothers and sisters to build some independence and dignity, self-hood and power of our own. From a timid bureaucrat toward an entrepreneur with *chutzpah*. From a stubborn but narrow liberal who praised nonviolent protest and the "activator vocation" because they might get the government moving (see my early articles in both sections of this book) toward an angry, more subtle, and more flexible radical who wants the people to take control of their own schools and factories, and learn to run them democratically—against the government. From a minor entry in a university directory, under orders (even from myself) to divorce social theory (learned in libraries during the day) from social action (undertaken in a Democratic Party club in the evening) toward a person with a growing sense of wholeness among knowledge and action, intellect and spirit, individuality and community.

I say *toward* in every case because I can feel that I am still moving; that every time the government runs riot out there, something runs riot inside me and I end up somewhere new. But this is where I am now:

The Super-States are the deadliest enemy mankind has ever had. They are on the verge of burning or poisoning the planet so badly that it cannot support human life, and far past the verge of reducing its poor to a state of hopeless fury. At the same time, they have created the possible seeds of their own dissolution: the transnational new class of those who have enough time and money to become free citizens (they are not free yet); and the science/technology that, although it is now utterly centralized and mostly destructive, could be transformed to serve democratically decentralized and life-giving work at a high level of income and leisure.

I believe that by the turn of the century (and millennium!) we may be living in one of four possible outcomes for Americans of this moment on the edge of the apocalypse: (1) the political destruction of all the new insurgent movements, and of freedom in America, by an alliance of blindly repressive corporations and military institutions, followed by the physical destruction of this continent into a desert through thermonuclear war or planetary pollution; (2) the rending of American society by an inconclusive civil war between the new class and underclass and some sophisticated Establishmentarians, on the one hand, and the old Establishment, most of the old working class, and most of the old small-business-oriented middle class

xi

on the other, accompanied by a steep decline in American wealth and power in the world and a collapse of the ability of the United States to pollute, destroy, or conquer the world; (3) the disorderly and uncomfortable, but basically peaceable, reform of American society under the leadership of a self-confident, knowledgeable, and vigorous Establishment prepared in its own self-interest to abandon the war machine entirely and use that money and knowledge to meet some of the demands of the old working class and old middle class together with the new class and underclass; and (4) the transformation of American society from the bottom by an alliance of the campus, the ghetto, the factory, and the office against any Establishment, whether hidebound or reform-minded, to build a democratic society of free citizens, able to unite productive work with politics and poetry.

I have put those possibilities in somewhat academic prose. To my heart and gut they mean these choices:

—my young son and daughter roasted to death in a thermonuclear firestorm engulfing Washington;

—their being shot or tortured by policemen after blowing up a chemical factory and killing 20 workers; .

—their growing up as bureaucrats in one or another corporation but getting their boss's permission to join as precinct legmen in a reform coalition, led by a latter-day Kennedy in the New Deal style, which wins world disarmament and the redirection of American resources to meet domestic needs;

—their spending a lifetime as organizers-workers-intellectuals building new institutions—a worker- and community-controlled factory that uses an advanced technology which does not pollute the streams and draws its electricity from a local power source, not a national corporate grid; or a transnational religious movement commanding so much more loyalty and dedication than the national government that it can offer asylum to a radical in trouble: sometimes in jail, sometimes in exile, ultimately dancing and singing in the park across from the White House, or from GM, or from Fort Jackson, as the old government dissolves and abdicates.

The difference between the third outcome and all the others comes from the possibility of the Establishment becoming effective, united, and forward-looking—which it is not now. The difference between the fourth outcome and all the others is in whether the Movement can reach out during the 1970s to new people from the "old" classes—factory workers, farmers, grocers, secretaries—and can build coherently.

But it should be clear: all four choices are a great departure from what we are used to. Even the third, which is most like the America I expected to live in when I came to Washington in 1959, requires a world without war—and that would be a major departure. (It begins to feel like the least likely result, too. To get there would require the most incredibly delicate balancing of social energies—energies that already feel as if they are blowing much too strong and furious to balance.)

But this is *not* all in the lap of the gods. Whether we act or not, and how, might make the difference. We have many emotional and intellectual journeys to take: many communities to build, many friends to cry over on the way to jail, many old articles and theories of our own to reject and rewrite, many nights in which to eat our hearts out over the collapse of some demonstration or organization. And many days to rejoice in our own sense of liberation and in the growth of something we suggested and in the abolition of a program we always said was evil.

*　　*　　*

I have said that this book represents a journey. Why on earth, then, is it divided into two parts, not chronologically but by a basic topic? Presumably a journey is a single complex process, one in which the traveler is jostled at successive steps by everything. Why then this neat division into one set of essays on the meaning and impact of the Black insurgency, and another on the meaning and impact of the peace-student-radical "new class" insurgency?

Basically because I am myself a "new class" insurgent who believes we must be very clear about a very difficult problem: our response to our own oppression, and our response to the worse oppression of others. To focus only on the one is to retreat into the politics of guilt and expiation; to focus only on the other is to retreat into the politics of greed. One of the deepest and most instructive torments of the radical is how to keep these responses both separate and together. I hope the successive essays in the two sections will show how I have tried to improve my ways of doing this. And the point is not only a psychological one: increasingly the world is moving toward a division between a Northern Hemisphere made up of fantastically rich and potentially democratic societies, and a Southern Hemisphere of the desperately poor under permanent autocratic rule. No radical who does not grapple with this division, from both directions, even begins to understand his world.

*   *   *

I have also said that where I am now is quite different from where I started. Why then should I inflict the ideas I had and the articles I wrote at earlier stages of this journey upon a busy public? What, in short, is the point of this book?

The point *is* the journey. The method. The hard, frustrating process of developing hypotheses about the uses and directions of power in America, using those hypotheses in action, finding them in part confirmed and in part confuted, and working out new ones. The baffling, infuriating, amusing process of intertwining history as change and history as record. Even the earliest of these essays still have—I think!—a lot of truth in them, and their very mixture of truth and falsehoods is—I hope!—a necessary part of understanding where we have been and where we are still going.

In addition, it is possible that the earlier essays, which assumed an intelligent Establishment at least moving to catch up with necessary change, will again become relevant to the real world. Although the likelihood of this outcome becomes less and less each month, I keep remembering that from 1929 to 1933 or even 1937, the American Establishment seemed to have turned its back upon intelligence; to have gambled away all its long-run stability in order to enjoy its short-run maximum power and wealth. Only deep in the Depression crisis did it decide it *had* to move because the pressures were too great. But then it really moved: not to abandon power to the insurgents, but to meet their most urgent bread-and-butter demands. Perhaps the Establishment is playing that game again; perhaps it is not yet convinced there is a real social upheaval going on, and when it becomes convinced will take swift and vigorous action. If so, those earlier essays may well be useful to liberals who find new space opening before them, space to live in without governing.

But it should be clear: for me that will not be enough. I believe that *we* should govern the space we live in. My head and heart have been permanently changed by my journey through the '60s, and I have glimpsed both the necessity and the possibility of a fully democratic society. That radical vision makes for a glorious trip, and as near as I can tell the drug is addicting. And dangerous.

*   *   *

I would not have been able even to begin the journey I have talked about if it had not been for communities of friends and colleagues, this past decade. From the moment I arrived in Washington and awkwardly set foot on Capitol Hill, I found that community with Marc Raskin. It was the love and help of Todd Gitlin and Carol McEldowney that made it possible for me—too old, too frozen, too conservative—to "join the movement." It was the sharing of energy with Marc Raskin, Dick Barnet, Sandy Jencks, Don Michael, and Milton Kotler that shaped the early days of the Institute for Policy Studies in such a way as to give us all space to think, work, fail, and breathe. It was such newer colleagues as Robb Burlage, Frank Smith, Judy Coburn, Ivanhoe Donaldson, Mariette Wickes, and Charlotte Bunch-Weeks who made me face some failings of the Institute and begin wrestling to move it, and myself, closer to a working radical community. It was a loving succession of students/comrades at the Institute, chief among them Jeremy Brecher, who made me analyze the tough political issues, make the tough political choices, that I often wanted to avoid. It was Sue Orrin, Larry Aaronson, Betty Garman, Sue Strauss, Bill Weiss, Mariette Wickes, Gerry Schwinn, Gabrielle Edgcomb, and Cynthia Ray who through the Center for Emergency Support taught me how to think and act collectively. It was an independent-minded, sardonic crew of Institute staff—especially Jackie Sue Thrasher, Tina Smith, Frankie Clark, Jan Hackman, and Cynthia Hughes, who have kept teaching me what "work" and "participatory democracy" meant. And it was Donald Jewell, Sheldon Kopp, and my wife Irene who urged me, forced me, enticed me, embraced me into beginning to open up to that world of inner feelings that I had always divided from my thought and action.

We will never survive unless we build such communities of thought, and work, and love, and action. We will never survive, either, if we build them in isolation and try to insulate them from confrontation with the riotous, reeling powers that now rule over us.

—AIW

I have just reread this book and this Introduction, and realized that I have not made clear—indeed, I suppose I have successfully suppressed—one important part of my life as a radical, these days. But I think it is important not to let myself suppress it.

I am frightened. Not just for America, but personally, "privately," for myself and my family. I was frightened by the murder of Fred Hampton, by the jailing of the Conspiracy, by the reports of the political use of torture in Brazil. And not only frightened—made to feel utterly helpless.

Every radical has his own particular nightmares these days—or nights. Most of the time we keep our nightmares to ourselves. And that is a mistake. For most of us are terribly and deeply lonely.

It is only in those moments when I am able to share with my brothers and sisters in the movement and my friends and colleagues outside it how frightened and lonely and helpless I feel—and they, with me—that my fear and loneliness diminish, my helplessness dissolves, and action becomes possible.

I have a hunch that most Americans feel this way, feel frightened and lonely and helpless, and "radicals" are just a little more conscious of it and a little more political about it. If we can share how bad it is with each other, maybe we can gather enough strength from each other to do what needs doing.

—AIW

RUNNING RIOT

Part I: White After Black:
From Sit-In to Mutiny

1
Why Jail?

At 11 o'clock on the morning of Sunday, July 7, 1963, I wrote the last paragraph of the last chapter of a scholarly study of a series of race riots that swept across the United States in 1919.* At 5:30 that afternoon, I joined several men and women, white and Negro, to enter a Baltimore amusement park, Gwynn Oak, which had forbidden Negroes to attend.

By 5:40, I had for the first time in my life met the kind of hatred and the kind of police partiality that Negroes meet in less concentrated form almost from their birth. One of my companions had been badly hurt by a thrown rock, and all of us had been surrounded by a raging mob that, as I could recognize from my study of the 1919 riots, was whipping itself up to the point of assault and murder.

Then the police arrived—to arrest my friends and me as trespassers, but not to arrest any member of the mob. (That pattern, too, I recognized from the 1919 race riots. Almost every one of those riots was precipitated, in a situation already heavily charged with racial conflict, by an act of police favoritism toward whites and against Negroes.) After that ten minutes, a sleepless night on cement floors in jail was an anticlimax. But it gave me time to start thinking about what I had experienced. I am still rethinking the whole business, but I have tried to set down here an "interim report" on my conclusions.

At bottom, I have been trying to clarify for myself why I left my research and writing to get arrested and whether I should have. Afterward, one of my friends wrote me that a scholar's brain is "too precious a national resource to be splashed on a ferris wheel." Is he right, or do moments come when only a scholar's willingness to splash his brains around can make his work and thought "authentic"?

* This article appeared in August 1963.

Most of the reasons I felt compelled to go were not directly related to my research. What stirred me most was my own sense of belonging to Baltimore and Gwynn Oak Park. I was born and raised in Baltimore, and I had ridden the roller-coaster and played miniature golf and danced around the ballroom at Gwynn Oak. My high school—it was still segregated then— held a June Week dance there. How could I sit around now, when a moral issue I had abstractly noticed in high school had become a burning question throughout the country?

More especially, how could I sit around while people who had only an intellectual interest in Gwynn Oak were going off to be arrested? For two students I knew in Washington—one from Ann Arbor, one from Harvard—had already marched off to jail on July 4. The friends and buddies that psychologists report soldiers really fight for—not for "the country" or "the cause"—evidently are the reason many nonviolent "soldiers" fight, too.

There were two more intellectual reasons that I went. On July 4 I had—as I've made a comfortable habit of doing every year—reread the Declaration of Independence. Then one of the clergymen who had "trespassed" that day explained he did so to celebrate the Fourth, and I realized how absurd it was to celebrate a revolution for liberty by reading about it, instead of joining it. And finally, one of the conclusions I had reached about 1919 was that riots exploded because no one had invented what might be called nonviolent "equivalents" of rioting. Now one such equivalent had been invented: the walk-in, a loving trespass. Wasn't it my business to advance what my own research said needed advancing?

So I went. I went without violence, but not "nonviolently," in the inward Gandhian sense. When the mob surrounded us, we faced them with more stolidity than love, more amazement than anger, and more curiosity than conscious courage. One of us had been badly cut by a thrown rock before the mob closed in, and our fear for her kept us from worrying about ourselves. Somebody in the mob yelled at us, "Yeah, you better look worried," and I remember wondering whether I really did. I also remember realizing that this mob was a great deal like some I had read about in my study of race riots, and that they were just at the previolence level. But my imagination was distant, remote, disconnected: I had no visual image of what would happen to me if they crossed the line into kicks and blows.

After the police had reached us and arrested us, I experienced the most vivid reinforcement of my sense of "belonging" to Baltimore and Gwynn Oak. Our march to the paddy wagon brought us past some of the same cotton candy stands and thrill rides that I could remember from fifteen years ago. I had a terrible flash of double vision; the same scene felt utterly different in this different emotional context, and yet I fully and physically realized it *was* the same scene. I felt utterly pierced by the knowledge that this was my Baltimore, the mob my fellow Baltimoreans, showing me hatred that I had never had to face, but that Baltimore Negroes must have faced for all their lives. This moment of double vision validated for me everything I had done. In some ways, it validated not only my act of protest but my decision five years ago to study race riots, and my decision last year to complete that study after several years away from it spent in analyzing problems of defense and disarmament.

But it has taken me several weeks to absorb even partially what this validation meant, and to work out what I had learned from it and from the whole confrontation at Gwynn Oak. For one thing, I gained an unexpected extra dividend in that whatever I think or write about conflict and violence will now have something new behind it: a feeling for what combat (armed or unarmed) is like, with its confusions of command and control (we got lost three times in looking for the back entrance to Gwynn Oak), its commitments to personal friends rather than "the cause," its suppression of both felt fear and felt courage in a kind of temporary "distancing." For another thing, I had taken into my guts what I had previously spun out only in my brain: that men were capable of sustained, focused hatred.

Still, these learnings did not answer the basic question: if I feel that scholarship and writing are important tasks for me to keep on with (and I do), what place should something like civil disobedience have in my life? Scientists get exempted from the military draft; should intellectuals be exempted from protest movements? I can't see why. Temporary deferments, maybe;

5

probably James Baldwin was more effective through *The Fire Next Time* than he would have been as one more body on the Freedom Ride. But, ultimately, it is dishonest to urge without undertaking, and impossible to understand without acting. In fact, the more cool and scholarly the intellectual side of one man's effort, the more necessary perhaps that the political side be hot and involved. Otherwise his books may well be a lot dryer and dustier inside than out, himself dryer than either, and his analyses a vague and useless guide to antiquarians.

Of course this does not mean the intellectual needs to be in jail all the time. What was most important to me about protesting at Gwynn Oak was that it grew out of what I had been, and done, and written, not just out of the newspaper headlines. I was prepared to go back to Gwynn Oak, but the management, under pressure of the demonstrations, agreed to integrate the park. With that issue, in which my life had been deeply involved, settled, I scarcely expect to be on the picket lines every Sunday. But where an event reaches out to touch my life again as this one did, I do not think I will be able to stay at my desk.

6

2
How to Avoid a Race Riot

The boiling pot of American racial conflict has given rise to widespread fear that hot weather may push the conflicts past the boiling point, touching off a series of race riots across the country.* There has been one such year in American history: 1919, when some observers counted about twenty-five racial clashes, of which seven were large-scale riots. In 1919 almost no one expected the riots; in 1963 almost everyone does, partly because of vague and buried memories of 1919. Bringing these memories to the surface and examining the 1919 riots carefully may indicate the reasons they occurred and suggest ways in which they could have been prevented—and perhaps ways in which potential riots this year may still be prevented.

As anyone who has read John dos Passos's *U.S.A.* will remember, 1919 was a year of upheaval. There was a general strike in Seattle, a series of Bolshevik scares, a bloody raid on the Wobblies at Centralia. But above all, there were the race riots that started the press screaming about a "new Negro."

In four of these riots—in Charleston, South Carolina; Longview, Texas; Knoxville, Tennessee; and Omaha, Nebraska—there was national publicity, but the fire was snuffed out before it got properly blazing. (In Omaha, the mayor was twice strung to a lamp-post and barely cut down in time, for trying to save a Negro from a lynch mob.) But in three localities—Washington, D.C., Chicago, and a rural area of Arkansas near the Mississippi border—the riots caused a number of deaths and took days to bring under control. These three cases are also interesting because the riots most clearly arose from the kind of underlying social conflict that is stirring trouble now.

* This article, written in the summer of 1963, summarized part of the scholarly study I had finished the morning of the Gwynn Oak walk-in, and applied it to the civil-rights struggle.

In Washington, federal job opportunities for Negroes had been reduced and segregation increased by the advent of the Southern-oriented Wilson Administration in 1913. Then World War I brought an influx of Southern whites to town, while Negroes suddenly found themselves earning more than they ever had and incurring white resentment because of their new prosperity. Into this atmosphere of anger and jealousy there came in the summer of 1919 headlines about a Negro "crime wave" and highly sensationalized accounts of rape and pillage.

Finally, on July 19, a series of nightly riots began. White mobs repeatedly tried to storm the Negro districts, Negroes fought back, and the local police kept arresting more whites than Negroes. Not until the much more nearly neutral men of the federal army—2,000 of them—had been brought in to police the city did the riot end, three days after it had begun.

By then six men had been killed, about twenty seriously injured, and dozens more hospitalized. President Wilson privately and Secretary of War Newton D. Baker publicly had expressed their concern, and newspapers all over the United States were demanding action—ranging from demands that uppity blacks get back in their place, to demands for the early elimination of school segregation in Washington, to demands for large-scale beefing up of the police, to demands that the police force be trained in the rudiments of racial impartiality.

The nation had scarcely caught its breath after the shock of rioting in front of the White House when a new race riot began, considerably longer and bloodier than Washington's. At a bathing beach in Chicago, on Sunday, July 27, an altercation erupted over the stoning of a Negro swimmer who had crossed an extralegal boundary into a "white" swimming area, and who drowned under the hail of stones. When a white policeman refused to arrest whites who were accused by Negro bystanders of having stoned the swimmer, and then arrested a Negro on a white's complaint of some minor offense, Negroes mobbed the white policeman. Reports of his behavior spread and aroused indignant Negro crowds. Gunfire broke out between Negroes and the police, and by nightfall white and Negro mobs were clashing in many sections of the city.

As the riot continued, the police were concentrated in the

8

Black Belt to control Negroes, so that few were available else-where in the city to protect Negroes from white marauders. Not until four days later, when Mayor "Big Bill" Thompson and Governor Frank O. Lowden finally agreed to have the state militia take over, was an impartial police force trying to con-trol the violence of both sides. Once the militia had arrived, the city calmed down quickly. But by then, 15 whites and 23 Negroes had been killed. That death rate was an index to the fact that among Negroes, there was already a new postwar spirit of readiness to defend themselves, especially among re-turning soldiers. National publicity for the Washington riot did its part. Instead of acquiescing in the "invisible line" drawn against them, or in police indifference, Negroes fought back. On their side, angry whites took the behavior of the police as a license to use violence.

The Arkansas violence began outside a Negro country church in Phillips County. Within the church a number of sharecrop-pers were discussing their dissatisfaction with the prices they were receiving for cotton sold through the plantation owners and with the prices charged them for supplies they were buying from the owners. The Negroes had organized a "Progressive Farmers and Household Union of America," and they were meeting to organize their campaign of action.

Arkansas whites charged that this organization was planning an "uprising." In a sense they were undoubtedly right—since a union of sharecroppers that gave Negroes in rural Arkansas equal bargaining power with whites would have constituted a revolution of sorts for Arkansas. But the charge that the union was a conspiracy for planning the mass murder of whites in the neighborhood was untrue, as was shown years later by whites who had been in Phillips County in 1919 and had helped concoct the "insurrection" story.

What really happened? Information on the Progressive Un-ion's plans to demand accurate accounts from the planters leaked out to the whites and alarmed them into using "every means they could apply" to force Negroes to leave the Union. On September 30 a fusillade of shots from outside were fired into the Hoop Spur church before any attack had been made upon the whites. To destroy the evidence of this unprovoked

9

assault, the church was burned next day by a large number of armed white men.

For the next several days after the clash at the church, white posses combed the canebrake, shooting down Negroes. Some shot back, but more were weaponless. By October 4, five whites and several times as many Negroes had been killed. Hundreds of Negroes were herded into jail, where a local committee of leading planters and businessmen screened them for "insurrectionary" behavior, ordered some released when their landlords vouched for them, and held the leaders of the Progressive Union on murder charges.

At the request of the Governor of Arkansas, the United States Army sent 500 troops into Phillips County in order to restore order. Their commander accepted without question the white version of events, but acted somewhat more impartially than the local sheriff and his posses. For example, he ordered both whites and Negroes in the leading town of Phillips County disarmed, and he ordered the jailed Negroes protected against possible lynch mobs. The presence of his troops had restored order by October 7, so that the county officials could tell "their" Negroes to stop talking and get back to work.

These three explosions, as different from each other as they seem at first glance, together point some lessons for preventing racial conflicts from turning into riots. In each of them, the trigger to violence was the unneutral action of the local police, and the most important factor in ending the riot was the intervention of a more nearly neutral outside force. If any single act is most likely to set off race riots in the summer of 1963, it is behavior by police that signals to whites that they are free to use violence against Negroes and signals to Negroes that they will have to defend themselves since the police will not defend them.

It would seem useful, therefore, for the President to concentrate on this point within the Administration, even while he is asking Congress for broader legislation. It is unlikely that riots can be averted simply by passing an equal accommodations act or similar laws intended to "get the Negroes off the streets and into the courts." For it is extremely unlikely that the Negroes

10

will get off the streets (even if the bills should somehow be passed by Congress). There is too much unfinished business— jobs, schools, housing—and no legislation that anyone can imagine being passed could establish racial equality in all these areas, all across the country. Now that Negroes know that going into the streets sometimes works, and indeed now that they know it *always* "works" in the sense that it restores their own feeling of manhood and independence, they will not be giving it up.

If the nonviolent demonstrations continue, and if the police in many cities continue to treat them as if they were armed marchers to burn down City Hall, there will be riots. For, again looking at the 1919 riots, it is easy to see that the thwarting of nonviolent means of protest forces violence upon those who are protesting. Thus the Arkansas sheriff treated the sharecroppers' union, a nonviolent means of carrying on conflict, as if it were an instrument of violence, and for his pains he got the violence he had presumably been trying to avoid.

For this reason the Administration, in addition to seeking legislation that would advance the broad goal of racial equality, would be well advised to work out strategy and tactics for dealing with the precise and limited question of preventing violence. As we have seen, that means keeping the local police impartial in general, and specifically keeping them from treating nonviolent protests as if they were violent.

There is already legal machinery available to serve this end, and the President need not even struggle with Congress to get the necessary legislation. Title 18, Section 242, of the United States Code provides:

Whoever, under color of any law, statute, ordinance, regulation, or custom, willfully subjects any inhabitant of any State, Territory, or District to the deprivation of any rights, privileges, or immunities secured or protected by the Constitution or laws of the United States, or to different punishments, pains, or penalties, on account of such inhabitant being an alien, or by reason of his color, or race, than are prescribed

11

for the punishment of citizens, shall be fined not more than $1,000 or imprisoned not more than one year, or both.

This passage has not so far been used to prevent local police, acting "under color of law," from interfering with peaceful public marches and demonstrations, or to prevent local police and judges from treating Negro pickets differently ("by reason of their race") than they would treat white labor unionists. There might be problems in trying to use Section 242 in this way. Problems would probably not arise where local firemen who have allowed other sorts of parades turn high-pressure hoses on Negroes who are peacefully demonstrating; in these cases, it would probably be possible to convict the firemen of breaking Section 242. The law could probably also be used against "instant arrests" like those in Jackson, where Negroes carrying American flags and picket signs were scarcely given a chance to step out of cars onto the pavements before being arrested. Such cases show clear discrimination "by reason of race" and probably also deprivation of rights of free speech protected by the First and Fourteenth Amendments. But what of cases in which the local police use local ordinances for controlling traffic to prevent large mass demonstrations that are actually interfering with traffic, or use ordinances against restraint of trade to arrest Negroes who organize boycotts? In other words, is it "unneutral" for police to prevent non-violent protests when such protests are in truth illegal under local law?

There are two answers to this question. First, if the aim of the federal government is to avoid riots, it would be wise to insist on the widest imaginable latitude for nonviolent protest, even if it should violate local laws. Secondly, if the Justice Department pressed these cases, the federal courts would simply have to decide whether each particular case was or was not a violation of Section 242 and whether local ordinances were being applied in such a way as to deny free speech or to discriminate by reason of race.

In any case, there is no reason for the Justice Department to delay the application of Section 242 in every case in which local officials frustrate nonviolent protest—even cases where the protests are actually interfering with regular community business. Indeed, warnings that Section 242 is to be applied might well deter many local policemen, firemen, judges, and other public servants from acting as they have been.

The result may be a series of nonviolent confrontations of power and morale, with some white citizens protesting against integration even as Negroes and whites protest against segregation. So be it. The alternative to such nonviolent confrontation is not the restoration of calm and a controlled society, as the President seems to think and to want. The alternative to nonviolent confrontations is riot.

For that reason, the President would do well to take into account these warnings that can be drawn from 1919 of *what needs to be done* to prevent riots. So far he seems to have learned only that riots might happen. He has—laudably—learned also that his weight must be put behind the belief in racial equality. But since there is no way to get Negroes out of the slums by Labor Day, his present program to deal with the possibility of riots is likely to fail. Immediate steps to insist on police impartiality and to protect nonviolent protest are urgently needed.

3
Counter-Insurgency at Home

When John McCone left his job as director of the CIA, he must have left behind in the files hundreds of secret reports about insurgent movements around the globe. As chairman of the California Governor's Commission to investigate the race riots in Watts last summer, he has now overseen the production of yet another such analysis. Since this one is public, we can now get a better idea of what was wrong with all the others.

For the Watts report is a disastrous failure of those highly political skills, empathy and imagination. Its tone is simple: *We* failed; *we* failed in the job of administering Watts, and the people there got angry at our maladministration. If *we* don't wake up and administer Watts better, *those people* down there will get angry again and burn our city down again. Worse. So *we'd* better give *them* more teachers, more buses, lots of retraining classes, and a big new hospital. It will cost *us* a lot, but it's worth it to *us* if *they'll* stop burning *our* city down.

This is the "good" face of counter-insurgency. The report does not recommend sending the Special Forces into Watts on a permanent basis, nor does it call for "military advisers" to the Los Angeles police force or suggest the use of napalm. It has the foreign-aid tone. But it is pretty clear that this is foreign aid. "We" run the city, Watts is "them." So far as the report goes, Mr. McCone and his colleagues had no feel at all for the very heart and nature of insurgency: that when people revolt they are demanding a share in running things for themselves—that they are demanding not only better lives but also the right to decide when, how, and what a better life is.

But this, of course, means a share of power. It is a highly political event, not merely a welfare demand—and there go

---

* This article, written in December 1965, reviewed the McCone Report on the Watts uprising: "Violence in the City—An End and a Beginning."

14

with it the classic "political" claims: that the police are oppressors, that The Law itself is unjust and may legitimately be violated. But to the McCone Commission, this meant only that, so far as complaints about the police were concerned, there was "a real danger that persistent criticism will reduce and perhaps destroy the effectiveness of law enforcement," and so far as civil disobedience of the law was concerned, that one important cause of the riot was "almost daily . . . exhortations here and elsewhere, to take the most extreme and even illegal remedies to right a wide variety of wrongs, real and supposed." In short, nasty and unreasonable "criticism" and "exhortation" were to be thought of as causes of the riot, not as symptoms—like the riot itself—of a demand for political power.

Let us examine in detail what the report has to say about the police—which are the focal point of all insurgencies:

> Chief of Police Parker appears to be the focal point of the criticism within the Negro community. He is a man distrusted by most Negroes and they carefully analyze for possible anti-Negro meaning almost every action he takes and every statement he makes. Many Negroes feel that he carries a deep hatred of the Negro community. However, Chief Parker's statements to us and collateral evidence such as his record of fairness to Negro officers are inconsistent with his having such an attitude. Despite the depth of the feeling against Chief Parker expressed to us by so many witnesses, he is recognized, even by many of his most vocal critics, as a capable Chief who directs an efficient police force that serves well this entire community.

And in order to deal with this problem (the problem of Negro criticism, obviously—not of police injustice), the Commission recommends, first, that the civilian Board of Police Commissioners get higher salaries, meet more frequently, hire more staff, and be more dedicated; secondly, that an Inspector-General be appointed within the police department under the authority of the Chief of Police, to review all citizen complaints

15

of brutality, corruption, or misfeasance; and finally, that police-men get more training in "human relations." Not a one having to do with a share of political power for Watts, in and over the police force. (The Inspector-General notion is not only an ad-ministrative gimmick, but is dishonestly defended as analogous to the I-G system in the armed forces. But the I-G in the Army concerns himself with internal Army matters, not with alleged injustices by the Army against civilians—except perhaps civil-ians in a conquered country under military government: Is that the model?)

Whatever happened to the notion that in a democracy, the police are immediately responsible to the citizens? That is a political notion, not an administrative one. In rural America, sheriffs are elected by every county. In metropolitan America, a neighborhood like Watts has more people than any rural county you can think of. Why shouldn't Watts elect its own police chief?

Or take the behavior of the police during the riot itself: Ac-cording to the report, leaders of various civil rights and Watts neighborhood groups proposed to the police on Thursday, after the very first night of small-scale rioting, "that Caucasian offi-cers be withdrawn from the troubled area, and that Negro offi-cers in civilian clothes and unmarked cars be substituted." These proposals were rejected by the Deputy Chief of Police because they were "an untested method" and ran "counter to the policy of the Police Department." This report is startling in itself, since Chief Parker was widely reported to have said dur-ing the riot that he had offered to pull his police out of Watts, and had been refused by the Negro leadership. But more im-portant, the Commission does not see the demand for neigh-borhood self-government implicit in this proposal, nor does it afterward treat this idea as worthy of being tested—since the "established procedures" that the police did use failed so abys-mally to keep the peace.

If the feeling that motivated the Negroes' request for with-drawal of the white policemen was the fear that they would act like a conquering army in Watts, then there is evidence to hint they were right—though the report does not examine it. It mentions that 34 people were killed. It gives no racial breakdowns, although the easiest way of assessing the amount of vio-lence coming from each racial group might well be counting the number of victims on the other side. (Certainly the Chicago riot of 1919, in which 23 Negroes and 15 whites were killed, 342 Negroes and 178 whites injured, and the Detroit riot of 1943 in which 25 Negroes and nine whites were killed, 197 Negroes and 219 whites injured, have been acknowledged the most nearly "equal," two-sided race riots in American history.)

But the trouble with that measure would have been what it revealed; for of the 34 dead in Los Angeles, 23 were killed by the police or the National Guard (evidently all Negroes), and eight more seem to have been Negroes—if one can read cor-rectly between the lines of the report. The only three whites killed seem to have been a fireman accidentally killed by a falling wall; a deputy sheriff killed when another sheriff's shot-gun was discharged in a struggle with rioters; and a Long Beach policeman whose death is left unexplained by the report. Of the 1,032 people injured, 773 were "civilians" (evidently over-whelmingly Negro, but there is no indication of this in the report) and 259 were policemen, firemen, Guardsmen, or other government officials (presumably all or overwhelmingly white). Those figures sound pretty onesided, a little more like a pogrom than either a riot or a Negro insurrection. Certainly the fact that the massive arson was carried on entirely or almost entirely by Negroes may be counted as redressing the balance in favor of seeing Watts as a two-sided riot; but how come Negroes with guns were so ineffective and policemen so bloody?

The report, having avoided the fact, can scarcely explain it. And it is probably the first report of a race riot in all Amer-ican history not to report the racial breakdowns of deaths and injuries.

Again, of the 2,278 felony charges filed against adults during the riot, 155 won acquittal and 641 "were disposed of prior to trial, primarily by dismissal." In other words, about one-third of the charges had too little evidence to support them in court. Why? The report has no explanation.

And again: throughout the riot, Chief Parker kept appearing on television with hostile, derisive, and contemptuous com-ments on the Negroes of Watts—culminating in his famous

17

"We're on the top and they're on the bottom." The people of Watts have TV sets. So every other news program during the explosive weekend itself, there was Parker on TV again, doing what no other police chief anybody can remember has ever done during a riot—talking where the rioters could hear him. (I was in L.A., and I saw him.) Since Parker knew he was anathema to Negroes, and since every sentence he said made him anathema the more, did it occur to him that he was inflaming the riot with every appearance? Evidently not. Did it occur to the Commission to rebuke him, or even to mention what he did? Absolutely not.

One final point. The Commission reports that there was no pre-planned instigation or central direction of the riot, but does point out that there is some evidence of organization and planning after the riot began. It mentions, in explanation, that large numbers of Molotov cocktails and handbills appeared during the riot. No further discussion. But this issue of leadership and organization would have been one of the most important questions of all, to anyone who saw the possibility of political thrust and meaning in the riot. *The Economist* of August 21, 1965, reported that a "War Council" of young men had formed after the first day of the riot to manage continued attacks and distribute assignments. Did the Commission examine that allegation? Perhaps, but if so, it made no report of its findings. But the members of the War Council, if it existed, were the "Negro leaders in Watts" that everybody was looking for during the riot. And if political change, political effectiveness, insurgency without riot are ever to become real in Watts, it will be the men who made up that War Council, or others like them, who will have to take the lead.

If they do, they will have to ignore or deny one crucial assumption of the McCone Report: the assumption that there are only two states of the political world, "law and order" on the one hand, and riot on the other. By attacking "disobedience to law" and "exhortations to take illegal remedies," the Commission made clear that it could see no distinction between riot and nonviolent civil disobedience. If the Commission and the rest of official America insist on that view, they will find they have a self-fulfilling prophecy on their hands. Only if new

18

forms of creative disorder can be invented in the Northern cities—forms of disorder that avoid violence and channel protest into effective change—will riots in the North be avoided. But those forms of protest will be disorderly because the Negroes of Watts and elsewhere are outside the system of order. They will include disobedience of law because the Negroes of Watts had no hand in making the law. They will express contempt for the police until the police have roots in and are responsive to the people of Watts. The disorder, the disobedience, the contempt need not be violent. But they will certainly not follow the rules of "law and order."

That is what insurgency is all about. In Los Angeles, or in San Domingo, or in Vietnam, or in the Congo. CIA take notes.

4

How to Prevent a Pogrom

What we are facing in our cities this summer is not a riot, not a revolution, only in part a rebellion; it is mostly a pogrom.*

Some would argue that the pogrom began—casually, sporadically—when the first Negroes were herded into the first Northern ghettoes to be harried by hunger, disease, and the police. And in a sense this is true. But as the dwellers of all ghettoes know, there is a life of suffering which may be called a permanent pogrom; and there is the *real* pogrom, the days and nights of terror when the police sweep down—once upon a time, mounted on horses with swords swinging; now mounted on tanks and helicopters, machine-guns firing.

The true pogrom has happened before, of course: it happened in 1917, when dozens of Negroes were killed in East St. Louis. It did not happen in Chicago in 1919 or Detroit in 1943—they were true riots, in which private mobs of whites and Negroes attacked each other, and about equal numbers of whites and Negroes were killed. It did not happen in Harlem in 1964—the violence there was by blacks against white property, and the city contained it instead of smashing it. But the day of containment is over; in 1965 Los Angeles tested out the pogrom which had been so long in disuse. That is to say, the violence in Watts was almost wholly between white police (rather than white mobs) and the Black community, and the dead and wounded were overwhelmingly Black. In 1967 we are watching that test bear fruit.

In late 1964, I could write hopefully of the replacement of race rioting by sit-ins. Why, in the two and a half years since then, has high conflict with low violence degenerated so quickly

* This paper was given as an address to a conference on "Washington's Hidden Riots" on Sunday, July 30, 1967, just after the Newark and Detroit rebellions.

20

into Newark and Detroit? I think we must blame a good deal of the reversal on the war in Vietnam. In 1964 the black community was promised an end to poverty, but in 1965 the expense of the war began chewing that promise to shreds. From 1961 to 1964, the official view of the United States government was that war was obsolete and disastrous, to be ended by world disarmament and replaced by the Peace Corps. But from 1965 on, our official view has been that violence used to advance whatever you believe in is legitimate—a belief that, stated over and over by our symbolic Monarch in the White House, permeates the ghetto and the police station as well. (Is it surprising that our worst periods of massive racial violence have been in 1863, from 1917 to 1919, in 1943, and from 1965 to 1967—all periods of war?) In 1964 there was a hope of jobs for the black community; but from 1965 on, under the impact of the war, such important parts of the civilian economy as housing faltered badly, and the only job available to many young men in the black community was that of soldiering—at the cost of death or wounding. So the war brewed anger in black America, and it brewed the belief that nonviolence was only a joke to be played by (and on) the black community.

The result: explosion after explosion, as the black communities tried to gather up their despair into their own two hands and shape it into a weapon that would end despair. And the only weapon that seemed available was violence. But even the violence has at first been directed chiefly at property rather than people: what some African nationalists have called "non-bloody sabotage." Once the looting and burning of property began, it was the white governments and police that began to use violence against persons. The first lives lost were those of looters and innocent persons who got caught near looters. It was then that black snipers began firing at the white police, killed and wounded a very few, and brought down upon their heads the furious escalation into military force. At any of these points, the white governments could have chosen to respond in any of several ways. The path they took of escalation led finally to ordering the National Guard and the Army into action, and these military organizations acted in fully military ways: indiscriminate attack on buildings and people, culminating in dozens of deaths

21

—including those of old men, women, and children. So once again we read the kinds of figures that signal a pogrom: 21 black men dead, 2 whites; 30-some black men dead, 3 whites. In a few weeks' time we could see recapitulated the whole nightmare of the Vietnam War: first try a little economic aid, and urge the local authorities to give the simmering peasants a bone of reform (the "summer programs"); then, when trouble erupts try counter-insurgency (the local police); finally, when the peasants shoot back, bomb the hell out of them. Shall we see next the "resettle-ment" of Negroes into well-policed "villages"? And where does *that* process end? The Black communities of America are not likely to settle for South African status.

America could take another tack. It could decide—black and white alike—that America is not a "white man's country" and that the great megalopolises cannot be governed from City Hall. America could decide that both power and money must be devolved upon the neighborhoods: the power to control their own police, their own schools, their own rehousing programs; and the money to do it with.

What would this require? In effect the building of new kinds of municipal governments, the remaking of the great urban metropolises into federations of neighborhood governments. But is this so overwhelming a departure for Americans? When the growth of the port of New York bashed up against the con-stitutional problem of the division of authority between New York and New Jersey, we did not wring our hands in despair, we created a new form of municipal government, the Port Authority. It might not even be impossible to create some kind of cross-federation of local black neighborhoods scattered across the Eastern Seaboard and the Great Lakes area: the Tennessee Valley Authority was in effect a regional federation of water- and power-users.

It is true that both TVA and the Port Authority brought power from the top down, and *that* is likely to be the crucial question for dealing with the black communities. Will the Super-New Deal response, the so-called "Marshall Plan" response, mean the creation of a Presidentially appointed Urban Reconstruc-tion Authority run *for* the black communities, not by them? If so, the results are likely to be as horrendous as those of urban renewal have been.

No, the need is for power to rest at and flow from the bottom. And let us admit it, *that* is the real trembling point for American society. Can we now insist that the structures of power and control that have shaped our great cities be reshaped to accept the demand for a share in the power to control the decisions that affect their lives that the black community is now making? I do not know, but we should be trying. We should be saying that the neighborhood school should be neighborhood run; that the people of Harlem have as much right to elect their own police chief as the people of Dane County, Wisconsin, have to elect their own sheriff; that the police on the beat in every block should be watched by the grass-roots equivalent of a Citizens Review Board (as, after the riot, the people of Watts began to watch and evaluate their police); that the public-housing projects should be run by the tenants and that decisions on urban renewal and rehousing should be worked out by the neighborhoods involved, not by the Mayor, the real-estate lobby, and the men in far-off Washington. When the neighborhoods are practically all black or all white, then their local governments will probably be, as well; in those few—precious few, but dear and precious—neighborhoods where a real community has been built across race lines (not merely the integration of one into the other, but the building of a new kind of community among them both), in those few cases, the local governments would be black-white mixtures and would be a model for the America we dream of some day. I hold the fragile hope that my own neighborhood, Adams-Morgan, may be one of these.

Are these proposals seventh-heaven politics? Are they revolutionary politics, to be achieved only by wrecking the whole metropolitan power structure in every big city—and therefore the national power structure as well? Leaving aside the question whether such a total transformation would be desirable in and of itself, I do not think that it is *necessary* to the achievement of neighborhood power. It seems to me that the urban Establishments have begun to realize that indeed New York *is* ungovernable—from City Hall. They have begun to talk about and

23

even in a few cases to experiment with decentralization. The urban Establishments (and their national connections) will of course not surrender even part of their power unless they must; but they are beginning to wonder whether they must.

It is the rebellions—the permanent rebellions of casual crime, desperation drug-taking, hopeless apathy—and the overt rebellions of the last several weeks that have made them wonder. And perhaps this brings us to the issue of violence. Is it necessary? Is it defensible? Is it wise? Even remembering that the status quo is violent (it condemns to death twice the proportion of black babies as white babies in their first year; it sends twice the proportion of black men as white men to die in Vietnam; are not these facts violence?), even so, is violence the only available or the most desirable response? And here I am talking about the initiation of outright and immediate violence against persons or property. I am not talking about self-defense, about sniping at National Guardsmen who are firing machine-gun bursts into your apartment house. In such a situation, the choices are probably to fire back, or surrender, and neither traditional American morality nor traditional American politics seems to require that people surrender. But the question of initiating outright violence is not so quickly answered.

I would argue that even if at a given moment it *seems* the only available response, the initiation of violence is not the most desirable and it is not necessarily the only response. I do not argue this from a religious or philosophical objection to all violence; and even if I did I would feel compelled to remember Gandhi, who believed that the dispossessed showed the highest courage when they used nonviolence but the next highest when they used violence, and who thought passivity before injustice was a worse behavior than violence. Nor do I argue this from the tactical calculation that if a minority uses violence, the majority will use worse violence upon it. Indeed, this second argument—for the tactical use of violence, built upon fear—was I think bound to be corrosive. For after using that argument for several years, SNCC discovered what Fanon had asserted: If one is to be free, one must not be afraid. Not even afraid to use violence, for fear that one would suffer worse violence in return.

But I am not convinced that one must *use* violence in order

24

to cast out one's fear of using violence. What if we could build a politics that eschewed violence not out of love, not out of fear, but out of a demand for the most effective means of seeking change? One might say nonviolence not as a philosophy, not as a tactic, but as a strategy. For probably the most successful way of pursuing change is to imagine a decent future and proceed not to plead for it but to build it—now. Now even if it is illegal now, as an integrated restaurant was in 1960. (But the sit-inners did not petition for new laws, they built the future in the present.) Or as a Black Democratic Party was in Mississippi in 1964. (But the Freedom Democrats did not simply petition for entry into the party, they built the future they envisioned—in the present.)

It is this process we need to pursue in the great cities. Black people want neighborhood governments where they can exercise power; they could build such governments before they are legal and use their existence to force them to become legal. Black people want police forces responsible to the Black communities; Black people could create them, work out how they should behave and what they should police (perhaps they should carry no guns, like the London Bobbies?) and use them whenever police were necessary instead of using the official "police" which are in fact an occupation army. And so on.

What role should whites who still see the American Vision play in this? First, they should be demanding that their governments, in which at present they have at least a formal voice, start decentralizing the metropolises. Secondly, they should be demanding that the huge amounts of money necessary for reconstruction of the cities be made available to the neighborhood institutions as they emerge. Third, they should insist that under no conditions should the local police, state militia, or federal forces be permitted to act like a conquering army. Far better to withdraw outside police from the Black communities and encourage emergency self-creating police to end the looting, as was done in Tampa—where it worked. And if it did not work, better to respond to looting by declaring a "free merchandise" day, throwing open the stores, and reimbursing the merchants, than by carrying on a pogrom. (It would not only be more decent, but cheaper.) Finally, they should be demanding an immediate end to the American War in Vietnam—the war which gave the

25

last turn of the screw to black despair and anger, which must take direct blame as the immediate cause of the recent violence, and an end to which would release the money, the political energy, and the nation-wide thanksgiving that would let us do what we need to do.

In the actual moments of violence, of course, these demands could and should be put forth, but it is hard to believe they would be accepted on the spot. Already white liberals and radicals have begun to work out ways of making clear their commitment to social change instead of repression, when violence comes. Lawyers—like those of the ACLU in Newark—have appeared in court on an emergency basis to apply for writs of *habeas corpus,* to get bail reduced, and so on. Various people have gathered and given away emergency food and medical supplies. We need to think through more such techniques: for example, physicians and nurses should not only treat wounds caused by National Guard attacks but proclaim to the world how they were inflicted and explain that the best medicine for them would be preventive. We might be gathering bail funds even in advance of violence, to be used for reconstruction projects in the black community after court appearances or, in case the violence never occurred, after a reasonable time. And so on.

Finally, a reminder of what we face. The kinds of social change that would have to be accomplished in order to end the rebellions or prevent their being turned into pogroms will not be undertaken quickly. So we have to expect that the rebellions-pogroms will continue, and the danger will grow that our rulers will unleash a merciless repression on the country. If we keep proposing, and acting on, a totally different response to the crisis, we may be able to keep that dark night from closing in upon us. We will have to do the job ourselves, without help from the centers of power. In some countries, it has been discovered after much travail that the Emperor was not wearing any clothes. In our country, the situation is even worse: for we learned the other night that the White House is empty. Given one of the great moments of social crisis in all American history, the man who is alleged to be President suggested we spend today in prayer. I am glad we are spending it instead hard at work

26

deciding what action to undertake. For as is well known, God helps those who help themselves.

There is an old saying, indeed, that God looks after children, drunkards, and the United States of America. But that was, I fear, in our more decent youth. For I suspect the relevant God today for Americans is the God of the angry prophets, the God of Jeremiah. It was that God who was haunting me two years ago when, in the first teach-in after our government escalated the war in Vietnam, I recalled that Jefferson had warned us, "I tremble for my country when I reflect that God is just." Two years later, our fear and trembling has turned to certainty and horror. Fresh from the blood of the children of Vietnam, we cannot expect Divine protection for ourselves. Now it is Lincoln, at another terrible moment of our past, whom we must remember: "If every drop of blood drawn with the lash shall be paid by another drawn with the sword, as was said three thousand years ago, so still it must be said, 'The judgements of the Lord are true and righteous altogether'."

Our empty President did not pray *that* prayer, though he should have. We cannot depend on anything but bankruptcy from the rulers of Washington. For that very reason, we must expect all the more from the people of Washington. Or, if indeed it has out of our horrifying history come to that, from the *peoples* of Washington: Black and white.

5
Black and White and Read All Over

On the morning of April 6, the *Washington Post* carried on page A-15 a photograph that in one breathtaking symbol summarized all of 1968 in America: a Marine standing alone behind a machine gun on the steps of the United States Capitol, the great dome rising behind him. The machine gun was pointed out at the people of Washington, some of whom had burnt part of the city down the day before.

Six months later there appeared a book* written by a dozen reporters of the *Washington Post,* containing 89 photographs—but not the classic one. Instead there is a picture of what seems to be the same Marine, still on the Capitol steps but now surrounded by pretty girls taking his picture. No machine gun. *No machine gun.*

First the reader boggles; then peels the onion of his mind, like so:

1. The machine gun has gone down the memory hole.

2. The second picture has no "meaning." A photograph of a gaggle of pretty photographers, plus one smiling Marine? Who cares? (Oh, that's interesting. All the girls are white.)

3. No, the second picture has *all* the meaning. Paint out the weapons, paint in the girls; the Capital is defended by love and apple pie, not violence; all is still well; even if Washington is burning *all is still well.* (All the girls are white? Well. Well, naturally under the circumstances . . . Yes, the second picture has all the meaning.)

4. No, the *shift* from the first to the second picture has all the meaning. The *Washington Post,* which managed that shift, has all the meaning. From day to day it softens the abruptness

* Ben W. Gilbert and the staff of the *Washington Post, Ten Blocks from the White House: Anatomy of the Washington Riots of 1968* (New York, 1969).

of conflict in its city. It depoliticizes, smooths over, avoids. The process is simply clearer when it is put together in a sizable study of a single event.

Not that this book is what would normally be called a "study." Most of it is a chronicle, almost a chronology, rather than an analysis. The only attempt at "sociology"—a statistical profile of those arrested—is based on 856 cases out of 7,600 arrested. The raw numbers seem adequate at first glance, but there is not the slightest indication as to possible bias in this one-ninth sample. Careful examination makes clear that it was not taken at random. Evidently no one under 18 and no one charged with a misdemeanor rather than a felony is included, but even within these boundaries only four-sevenths of those charged are described, and there is no way to tell whether those not included are quite different in some crucial way. So we learn nothing of value about those arrested—or rather, we are left ignorant of whether we have learned anything of value.

Almost all the rest of the book is simply a rehash of the stories the *Post* published during and after the uprising itself. So patent is this that many of the reporters who worked on the book have privately expressed their considerable disappointment with the result. They are not sure whether to blame Ben Gilbert, the senior author, who is deputy managing editor of the *Post,* or Praeger—the publisher—for the fact that many hours of their effort went down the drain. They define the book's failure on two levels: its superficial chronicling of the hourly events of April, and its backing away from such political issues as criticism of the city government of Washington. (The two may be connected: it is easily possible that any analysis would have entailed criticism, whereas a somewhat sensationalized chronicle of the uprising might make best seller stuff and certainly would require no sharp examination of city politics.)

Item: reporters were asked to check on whether there had been any sabotage of public utility services during the uprising, did some careful research, and then had their results ignored.

Item: at least two chapters written by reporters at considerable personal effort were totally rewritten, with analysis omitted.

Item: factual details were "improved on" for the sake of sen-

29

sation. (For example, mud that was actually ankle-deep at Resurrection City became "hip-deep" in print.)

Item: reporters did depth interviews with various black leaders and activists on the meaning of the April uprising, not one of which was used in the book.

Item: one reporter's careful historical study of the degree of anti-Semitism among black militants through the twentieth century (conclusion: extremely little) appears nowhere.

The book, in fact, is no more a community effort of equal journalists sharing their concerns and discussing their information with each other than the *Washington Post* is every morning. Nor is the book a platform for individualistic "academic freedom" among reporters—indeed it is less so than is the *Washington Post* each morning. Either of these models—communal product or platform for free individuals—might have made for a book with analytical and political bite. But the book is instead a one-shot no-byline newspaper: information gathered by the hired hands, rehashed and served up by rewrite men, reviewed by an editor for political orthodoxy, and—perhaps—finally shaped by the publisher. Caveat: this is therefore not a *book,* if a book is the freely worked version of the authors' views and research.

Politically, the book carries on the *Post's* protective concern for the city's "Mayor," Walter Washington. (Though Washington is appointed by the President and is legally called Commissioner, the *Post* has since his appointment called him "Mayor" and treated him as if he were the elected representative of the people of Washington.) For example, the book describes decision-making during the riot:

> During the occupation of the capital city, the Mayor, Presidential trouble-shooter Cyrus Vance, Task Force Washington's Commander General Ralph E. Haines, Jr., Public Safety Director Pat Murphy, and their aides spent most of their waking hours in the police headquarters' command center, down the hall from the Task Force Washington "war room"—where a large wall map of the city showed trouble spots and troop concentrations.
>
> Deputy Mayor Thomas Fletcher said later that the

30

decisions made during the occupation of the city "were all done around the table," in the office of Police Chief John B. Layton. "Cy Vance was always there with the book he prepared after Detroit."

The "book" contained the lessons learned from the mistakes made during the 1967 riot in Detroit, where Vance served as the President's special representative. Vance was in on every major decision, always suggesting or questioning, rather than ordering, and getting along very well with Mayor Washington and ranking police officials.

But most reporters, a number of city officials, and private persons such as clergymen involved in relief work have reported that Vance was the key decision-maker; that he "got along very well" with Washington and the police because he was polite in making clear what should be done, and because they did not assert any claim to real authority. Indeed, the situation would have been clear enough if the locale had been British India or the time 1775: the colonial Governor-General of the city had not been able to prevent an uprising; the Emperor downtown had replaced him with an emergency Viceroy whose previous experience had been management of the Imperial military forces; the regular Governor-General was called in to supply information and keep the correct telephone lines open. But the *Post* could not see things so clearly in its own bailiwick.

Take another example: the book describes a food-relief operation run by the churches, then delicately says that the "food distribution machinery was turned over to the city's Welfare Department, which wanted to 'professionalize' it. As the professionals moved in and the amateurs moved out, it soon became clear that the welfare workers were not as well prepared as the volunteers. It took a couple of days . . . to work out the kinks. To some welfare workers, 'professionalizing' meant making sure that only 'deserving' persons received food."

No hint here of the hot political argument that broke out between the church leadership—hardly radical, but shaken by the specter of suffering—and Winifred Thompson, director of the Department of Public Welfare—probably the city official most

31

hated by the black community—over direction of the relief effort. No hint here that the Welfare people explicitly were angry that free food might be going to people who "didn't need it," although the churches were convinced that floods of free food would quickly swamp any profiteering that might emerge, while meeting the real needs of those who had lost their corner store and those who had been chronically hungry before the uprising. No hint here that Walter Washington sided with Miss Thompson and the Welfare Department. No hint here that he also sided with the police, who wanted to get suburban whites and middle-class blacks off the streets instead of letting them keep on delivering food to churches—for fear that policemen who took the curfew too seriously might arrest some politically in-digestible Senator's wife carrying groceries into town. In short, no hint of any political clashes—though the uprising heightened, rather than reduced, the real political conflicts in the city.

The one area in which the book reports a political and ideological conflict in some detail is the one over the behavior of the courts—in the chapter on "Fair Trial." There it becomes clear that both white and black libertarian lawyers and the families of those arrested believed that abandonment of normal bail procedures, delays in "processing" prisoners, and the seeking out of conservative ABA lawyers as defense attorneys while blacks and liberal whites were kept at arm's length were devices used to protect "security"—that is, property—in the city, at the cost of constitutional liberties. (Even this chapter does not dis-cuss the argument of more radical lawyers that the whole curfew system was an unconstitutional attempt to deal with the dif-ficulty of distinguishing and apprehending "real" criminals by defining non-criminal activity such as walking on the street as a crime, and then arresting everyone in sight. Nor does it mention the argument put forward by some black militants and white radicals that under the conditions of American racism, "looting" was not criminal behavior at all.) Why the willingness to discuss open conflict with the courts, but not the city government? Per-haps partly because the anger of liberal lawyers became public knowledge, whereas the fight over food relief became known to fewer Washingtonians—so omission of the court fight would have been widely noticed and the other not. But it is also hard to avoid the notion that the presence of Walter Washington in or his absence from the situation may be the important variable.

But why, then, is the *Post* so careful of its "Mayor"? Reporters tend to cite Ben Gilbert's close personal friendship with Walter Washington to explain not only the kid gloves in this book, but also the *Post's* tenderness throughout the year. Many reporters say they have had paragraphs critical of Washington excised or softened. (One said he could roast Mayor Daley for the use of tear gas in Chicago, but not Mayor Washington for its use in the District of Columbia.)

But the problem may lie deeper than personal friendship. Walter Washington's role as a black cushion between black anger in the city and the white business-government alliance which really rules the city may be an important one for the liberal managers of the *Post* to protect. On the one hand, it leaves them free to criticize the harsh exactions of an invisible establishment while praising the futile efforts of a powerless appointee to moderate them; on the other hand, it allows them to criticize the sharp demands from black activists for a fully democratic reconstruction of the city, while praising the moderation and perseverance of the black appointee. If the establishment and the insurgents came face to face without a cushion between, the *Post* might have to choose sides publicly—and choosing full democracy would endanger its own interests. (The *Post* is, next to the Federal government, the largest employer in the city.)

The *Post* not only has an investment in playing up Walter Washington, the symbol of black-and-white-together liberalism; it has a complementary investment in playing down the existence of black-and-white-together radicalism. Indeed, *Ten Blocks from the White House* veils from sight the bare existence of white radicalism in Washington. For example:

There is no mention of the fact that about 70 faculty and students (mostly from American University) picketed the White House just as the city began to burn, mid-afternoon of the day after King's murder, with a demand that the Army and the police be kept out of the black community and creation of a neighborhood-based police be encouraged instead; that about 40 of these picketers crossed to the White House side of Pennsylvania Avenue in defiance of a police ban; that they were charged, knocked down, and beaten by the police; and that three of them were arrested.

There is no mention of the fact that almost all of the whites arrested for breaking the curfew were young, long-haired, "hippie-looking," and politically radical; that reporters from the *Washington Free Press* (the underground paper) were arrested for breaking the curfew even though all had press credentials and one of them a police pass; that some white "hippies" joined in the "looting" both because they needed the food and because they viewed the whole social system—and especially the sale of food for profit—as illegitimate.

There is no mention of the fact that some white radicals kept on distributing food even after the churches had given up and they had been threatened with arrest for curfew violations.

Of course the number of white insurgents during April was small, compared to black insurgents and to fearful white defenders of the status quo; but how astonishing—how newsworthy!—that they existed at all. But the book ignores them.

It does even worse in describing post-riot development: it specifically defines the proposal for neighborhood control of the police through elected precinct commissions as an issue "dividing black and white"—though numerous white groups joined the Black United Front in supporting the proposal.

In short, *Ten Blocks from the White House* is not a neutral "anatomy" of the April uprising in Washington, as its title claims. It could not possibly have been one, because there is no such thing as an anatomy of history or society: there are only dynamic physiologies, and they are not neutral because their writers do not stand outside the body politic. But what is disastrous about the book—and about the *Washington Post*—is that it claims to be and tries to be an anatomy, a recitation of the names of muscles and bones with no special social or political interests of its own. That is the worst unneutrality of all, for it draws the veil of illusion across the reader's face—instead of clearing his vision as the explicit and self-acknowledged political actor does. The need is for reporters who know and editors who acknowledge their paper's bias, who understand their paper as a political institution like any other in their city.

And more: who report it that way.

6

Towards Community Control
of the Police

In almost every American metropolis, the police are no longer under civilian control—that is to say, democratic public control. Whether it be constant harassment of Black youth in Los Angeles and white youth in Washington, the brutal repression of white dissidents in Chicago and the beating of peaceful Black Panthers in New York, the refusal to obey orders of a black mayor in Cleveland and a white president of the Board of Education in Philadelphia, or the failure to answer routine calls for assistance from black neighborhoods of Detroit and white neighborhoods of Baltimore, it is clear that there are many people in the metropolitan areas who do not believe they can make the police respond to their needs. The problem is clearer and more chronic in Black neighborhoods and the consciousness of it is clearer there (so that it is seen not as a "failure" but as the successful carrying out by the police of the mission of being an occupation army). But parts of the white community—the young; dissident middle-class liberal peaceniks; even such Establishments as those that try to set up civilian review boards; even such ethnic working-class communities as those that threw rocks at Martin Luther King's Chicago marches—feel unable to control their police. Increasingly, the police control themselves.

There are two ways they do so. First, by constructing a police subculture of life-long policemen they insulate themselves against informal social control—defining their own norms; defending, rewarding, and promoting policemen who adhere to these regardless of public pressures or orders from above; insisting that policemen are "professionals" who should be trained by "professionals," so that civilians are increasingly excluded even from police academies. (They have been strongly abetted in creating the "professional" subculture by the efforts of liberals to "up-grade" and "professionalize" policemen into gentler behavior.) Secondly, they have, on the basis of this subculture, organized quasi-unions with considerable political clout, which have been able to "negotiate" practical autonomy on most occasions and when that has failed have been able to take on traditionally powerful groups (like the combined Democratic and Republican leadership of New York City plus the "civic" leadership plus most of the church and ethnic organizations, in the fight over a civilian review board) and win.

The process of establishing the political autonomy of the police has been similar to that which democratic societies have traditionally dreaded in connection with military services—that is, the emergence of a "Prussian" professional military—and has gone hand in hand with the police forces' increasing definition of themselves as para-military bodies. But until very recently, it has not inspired in the general public anything like the same kind of horror that feared breakdowns in civilian control of the military have. This is probably because the lack of civilian control has been clearest in the relation of the police to the least powerful communities in most large cities (especially the poor, the black, and Spanish-speaking communities), and only recently have elements of middle-class communities found themselves power-less vis-à-vis the police.

During the period from the 1940's to about 1965, when liberal criticism of the police focused on "brutality" toward Black people, the liberal solutions were psychological screening to exclude sadists; human relations training to soften racial "prejudice"; professionalization to reduce "lower-class" or "un-trained" reliance on naked violence; and civilian review boards to discipline particular violators of professional norms. All have failed. Among the most "professional" big-city forces has been that of Los Angeles; among those most carefully screened to ex-clude sadists has been that of Chicago; among those with a "strong" civilian review board has been that of Philadelphia. The review board especially merits study; it seems to have failed be-cause it triggered intense opposition from the police without at the same time mobilizing any real political base for itself. (It was seen as a "neutral" body of notables, above the battle; and the groups it was intended to protect, such as the youth and the black community, have responded coolly.) The review board has also been unable to (and was not intended to) go beyond particular instances of brutality or harassment to the deeper questions of what policemen were, what they were intended to do, what priorities in law enforcement they should follow, and so on. It could not even address evils of omission.

For these reasons, it seems urgent to go much deeper into changes in the institutional structure of police departments and in the very nature of the police career, if there is to be any serious change in police behavior. The evidence suggests that much more real change was achieved by such efforts as (a) the Community Alert Patrol in Watts, where citizens accompanied the police day and night and took notes and photographs of their behavior; (b) the Crusade for Justice in Denver, where Mexican-Americans chose their own civilian review board which investigated charges of police misbehavior and brought political pressure to bear whenever it believed grievances to be real and legitimate (as a labor union does in its grievances procedures); (c) the "white-hat" phenomenon in Tampa, Roxbury, and elsewhere, in which black communities were encouraged to police themselves, the outside police were withdrawn, and ordinary citizens—teenagers, clergymen, and so forth—took over the neighborhood police function. Most of these efforts were temporary emergency measures only, but they indicated what might be possible on a long-term basis. (But it should be recognized that on a long-term basis, they would mean much more real and basic change than they did as emergency measures—and the resistance will therefore be greater.)

There are at least three major possible directions that might be taken to achieve change in police forces of the kind that seems necessary and to restore democratic civilian control over the police:

1. Formal restructuring of metropolitan police departments into federations of neighborhood police forces, with control of each neighborhood force in the hands of neighborhood people through election of commissions.

2. Creation of countervailing organizations (in effect, "trade unions" of those policed) responsible to a real political base, able to hear grievances and force change.

3. Transformation of the police "profession" and role so as to end the isolation of policemen from the rest of the community, and thus to establish *de facto* community control by chiefly informal means.

1. NEIGHBORHOOD CONTROL

The "neighborhood control" approach could be institutionalized by election of neighborhood or precinct commissions which would (1) appoint high precinct officers (perhaps with approval of metropolitan headquarters, the mayor, or a civil service commission); (2) approve the assignment in the precinct of new policemen, and be able to require transfers out; (3) discipline officers, perhaps with concurrence of a city-wide appeal board; (4) set basic policy on law enforcement priorities in the neighborhood.

Such an arrangement would respond first of all to the possibility that no great metropolis can be democratically governed from City Hall: that departments of education, police, zoning, and so forth may necessarily become far too bureaucratic and too insulated from popular pressures and fresh ideas if they try to govern from one center a public of more than 100,000 people. It would thus accept the tradition of rural counties and suburban towns that find electing the sheriff or closely supervising the town police is workable. Secondly, "neighborhood control" would respond to the concentration of the Black populations in particular neighborhoods, and would thus attempt to deal at least with the "occupation army" aspect of a white-governed police force in Black areas. It might also make working-class ethnic neighborhoods and middle or "new class" neighborhoods more able to shape their own police forces, and might even provide a framework for dealing with the difficulties that the "youth minority" has with policemen. (One of the Washington, D.C., proposals for neighborhood control provides that of a seven-man board, one be a policeman elected by the neighborhood, one be a City Councilman designated by the Council, two be between 18 and 25 years old, elected by that age group, and three be over 25, elected by that age group. Thus the youth minority would have a "legitimate" voice in controlling the police—a power it now tries to exercise "illegitimately" through constant confrontation.)

So far as the Black neighborhoods are concerned, elected precinct commissions with the powers described would make possible great changes in the policemen who walk or ride the beat. Policemen might be chosen from the neighborhood and required to live in it. Black recruits are far more likely to appear if the police did not in fact bear the stigma of an occupying army, and are far more likely to feel and act like members of the Black community when they are no longer under pressure from a white-bossed headquarters and overwhelmingly white colleagues. Neighborhoods where back yards and recreation cellars were scarce might decide that enforcement of laws against playing ball in the alley or loitering to talk on the street would not be high-priority matters, and that enforcement of laws for decent housing would. Policemen would be much more likely to take seriously and answer promptly calls for their help. Drunks in the inner city might be taken home to their families like drunks in the suburbs, instead of beaten mercilessly and dumped in jail. The cries of "Nigger!" and "Boy!" would be much less frequent. The Black community would almost certainly be living much more comfortably with its police.

The idea of neighborhood control of the police has been objected to on two related "territorial" grounds: that major differences in style of law enforcement could plague any one person as he moved around the metropolis, and that "hot pursuit" questions (and other similar negotiation problems of the neighborhood forces) would be much worse. Both these "difficulties" exist now in rural and suburban jurisdictions, and can only be said to be new in the sense that population density might make a difference. It is true that shifts from one neighborhood to another come more quickly than from town to town, that more people do in fact move from one neighborhood to another during their daily lives. But it should be noted that already, in a city like Washington where U.S. Park Police, Capitol Police, White House

Police, and Metropolitan Police have major geographically distinct jurisdictions within the District of Columbia, solutions for "hot pursuit" and similar problems have been worked out. And so far as the problem of different styles in law enforcement is concerned, it seems already true that within a single city there are great differences from neighborhood to neighborhood, especially in the regulation of street conduct—but they are defined by policemen, not the public.

It might be objected that neighborhood control of the police does not go far enough, since other institutions are so closely connected to police functioning. For example, would neighborhood control of at least the small-crimes and small-claims courts be necessary, in order to uphold the meaning and usefulness of neighborhood control of the police? Perhaps in part, the logic would move in this direction. But note that neighborhood control of the police is not utterly meaningless without similar control of the courts: the police are themselves the court of first resort. If they do not arrest, there is no trial; if they arrest people and punish them physically or by keeping them away from work or damaging their reputations, there has been a *de facto* conviction and punishment without trial.

Conversely, would neighborhood control of the police destroy some city-wide institutions that ought to be protected? Not necessarily: for example, such police divisions as fingerprint and *modus-operandi* files, a homicide or arson squad, and so on, could still function under metropolitan police headquarters.

Finally, would neighborhood control in itself—regardless of the decisions made by the elected commissions—require changes in the role of the policeman? Perhaps the most politically ticklish question would arise around the function of the policeman as protector of property. In neighborhoods filled with property owners, that role would be supported; but in neighborhoods of the poor, would the residents put great store on the protection of property? It is precisely the fear that they would not that has motivated many property-holders to insist that the poor should be policed by outside authority, rather than police themselves. What if they did police themselves?

Several resolutions of the "problem" seem possible—depending on the balance of political energies and beliefs in the cities and the nation. First of all, the poor might turn out to want their few miserable possessions protected as desperately as the rich want their great hoards. The poor might even be prepared to say that all property—that of the wealthy as well as their own—should be protected. The present ideological commitment of the middle class to protect giant property that it does not own suggests that for long-range reasons, intelligently or stupidly conceived, people will protect even interests that in some ways damage them. The poor might conceivably, given neighborhood control of the police and the end of the rawest racial indignities, join with the middle class on this matter. Secondly, the society might transfer control over at least some property at the same time it transferred control over the police, so that neighborhoods of the poor would own important kinds of property—perhaps collectively through coops—and would therefore have as strong an interest in protecting it from individual marauders. And finally, it would be possible to decide that police should not protect property—at least where doing so endangered persons. Stolen or damaged property could be replaced through a kind of public insurance, and neighborhoods of poor people might decide to give the police a new charge, specially oriented to serving the propertyless: "advocacy of change," in which the policeman becomes like a community organizer/attorney. For example, the "policeman" might lead challenges to illegal housing practices in tenements owned by outside slumlords.

Which of these directions the police relation to property might take in Black neighborhoods would depend on the level and kind of organizing work that was going on there. In the usual kind of paradox, Establishment figures who oppose neighborhood control of police because the sound of crashing glass in downtown department stores fills up their nightmares are likely to delay its arrival long enough that anger at them builds up. Then, assuming that neighborhood control of the police is finally achieved, a radical political outlook unfriendly to big property is more likely to have great resonance in the ghetto. The sooner neighborhood control is granted, the more likely the neighborhood will be conservative.

41

2. COUNTERVAILING POWER

The possibility of control of the police through counter-vailing power is based on two recent models: the emergence of the Community Alert Patrols in Watts and elsewhere as checks on the police, and the Community Review Board created by the Mexican-American community in Denver. Both are vastly different from the conventional neutral Civilian Review Boards, in that they are explicitly based not on a quasi-judicial model but on the necessity of having independent political power to confront that of the police forces. Both assume that the police are themselves either an independent political force or an arm of a powerful establishment, not a neutral peace-keeping body.

Thus both approaches seek some external political support for pressing grievances against the police. In the Denver case, *chicano* organizations investigate charges of illegitimate or unjust police behavior and, where they regard the charges as well-founded, demand punishment of the officers and back up their demands with political pressure (publicity, threatened loss of votes, threatened disorder, and so on). As for the CAP arrangements, they used the endemic anger of young Black men against the behavior of the police in the black community to energize youth patrols, accompanying the police on their rounds to take detailed notes and photographs of their behavior. Where the patrols felt the police acted badly, they filed complaints and sometimes tried to turn on some political heat to achieve redress. The Watts CAP tried, notably, to combine the insurgent political energy of the black community with the outside political (that is, financial) support of the Federal government, and thus to box in the police force. But what the Watts CAP hoped to gain from the Federal tie in political ability to resist enormous hostility from the police, was lost in the weakening of ties with the Black community itself. The CAP's legitimacy within Watts declined; and then, when the Los Angeles Police Department brought its political power to bear, the Federal government backed off.

The major lessons to be learned from previous experience

42

with the CAPs are that they must be financially and politically responsible to the aggrieved constituency, and that some institutionalization of this responsibility is essential so that the community can remove any CAP men that have stopped being the community's representatives. Although financing such an institution from poverty-stricken neighborhoods is not easy, the existence of such groups as the Black Panther Party in Oakland (which has at least asserted that it would like to exercise some of the function of reviewing police behavior) suggests that it is possible. It might be possible to create an open-ended community group that anyone in a given police precinct could join, the directors of which would be periodically elected, and that would be able to hire a staff of investigators (perhaps some full-time and some part-time) to watch over the police in that precinct. Such a community group might even, if the neighborhood energies were vigorous enough, be able to accept foundation or government grants without compromising itself —but independent financing would be better.

Such an organization (if it proved feasible) would probably not challenge the basic assumptions behind present-day policing, but would from its very nature as a grievance-processing institution tend to assume that only particular "errors" or grievances needed to be dealt with. Only if such a group saw grievance-processing as an interim responsibility leading to replacement of the regular police with an indigenous group would it be likely to raise basic questions about the nature of police work. (In short, many of the same issues raised by bread-and-butter unionism as against socially conscious or even syndicalist unionism would be raised in this context.)

The countervailing-power approach may have some advantages over neighborhood control. Perhaps the major one is that it can be undertaken without the agreement of those in power, whereas the neighborhood-control model requires governmental acquiescence. It should also be noted that it does not need to be tied to a neighborhood base. Where a given community that feels itself the powerless object, not the defining subject, of police power is scattered across a city—or where political feeling of this sort is not sufficiently strong in any single neighborhood to support a "union" there—then a countervailing organization along the lines of the Denver Crusade for Justice could be useful. And finally, some activists have argued that at least in the short run it is wiser to organize the powerless to oppose police power than to grasp it—on the ground that power over one police precinct, or even many, in the absence of drastic social change in other spheres of life may simply make fuzzy the face of the enemy, require the poor to police themselves in the patterns demanded by the unchanged spheres of social power, and thus stultify movements for more basic change. In this sense, organizing "against" and refusing to take control of any traditional "legitimate" institution until there is about to be over-all social change may keep the situation clearer and more real. Whether this analysis is correct may depend on whether the police are in fact a central or merely a peripheral institution, and therefore whether taking control of them changes everything or leaves everything the same.

3. TRANSFORMATION OF POLICE ROLES

As we have suggested above, the isolation of the police into an angry and frequently frightened subculture with a tight and effective political "face" is at least as important a factor in preventing democratic control as are the formal command hierarchy and its ties to the metropolitan white power structures. These informal anti-community factors are especially important in the relation of the police—who are overwhelmingly recruited from the old working class and lower middle class—to the Black underclass and the white "new class" of the campus trained. So it may be just as important to work for community control by cracking this informal "blue curtain" as it is to change the formal power relations and command hierarchies.

In the examination of ways to crack the "career" subculture, an important distinction should be kept in mind: the distinction between on-the-street peacekeeping and the more formal and "organized" policing of systematic off-street crime, as quite different roles of people we call "policemen."

In the first case, it seems relatively easy to argue that the police should not be "professionals" or career men. The role of peacekeeper on the beat is not a highly technical or specialized one, but depends rather on a somewhat widespread and certainly non-professional skill in conciliatory human relations. The "false professionalization" of the role is due in part to an effort by policemen to defend their jobs and careers, and in part to the attempt of middle-class liberals to "upgrade" and "retrain" working-class policemen, on the theory that "the uneducated cop" was typically brutal or racist. This process could be reversed. Peacekeepers could be recruited for a term of not more than three years from a broad cross-section of the public —especially, and deliberately, from among women as well as men and from a wide age range, so as to emphasize the peacekeeping rather than the force-dispensing function. Such peacekeepers would probably not carry firearms, but would probably be trained in such defensive tactics as judo. They should probably wear uniforms quite unmilitary in style, be required to live in the community and keep up strong social contacts in it, and so on. Thus the community should see them as quite unlike traditional "policemen," and this perception should be accurate. Their command line should be totally divorced from that of the regular "police" department, and ideally would run to a neighborhood commission of the kind described above.

The short term might prevent the rigidification of a police culture and police political power. There might be a danger of large "veterans" organizations, but the chief danger of military veterans groups comes from their origins in and ties to an officer cadre which would not be present in a deprofessionalized on-the-beat police force.

If it is true, as has frequently been claimed, that those who volunteer for police duty are specially self-selected for tendencies to sadism and so forth, then even a short-term volunteer process might not change the police enough, and one might have to think about selection of police by lottery from the whole population, or some similar means. But most of the evidence suggests that recruitment for the police proceeds on so many different appeals that if sadism is widespread, or becomes widespread on particular occasions, that is because it is learned on the job from other officers and from the nature of the role. If that is so, reducing the "career" line to three years would greatly weaken the informal social pressures from older policemen, and transforming the role would change the direction of the pressures.

The peacekeepers would deal with such traditional worries of the patrolman as family fights, conflicts between a tavern owner and unruly customers or between sleeping old people and singing youngsters. Indeed, some police authorities say patrolmen spend 80 % of their time on such matters—and resent it terribly. For they are taught that their function is to Enforce the Law, not calm people down. Thus they tend to be bad at what they feel is a waste of their time and training—and of course even worse at it when they are strangers to or contemptuous of the community they are doing it in. Peacekeepers who are recruited for that precise job would do it better.

Meanwhile, alongside the transformation of the neighborhood street police, there should be a re-examination of the "downtown" policemen. Here there are two issues: should these men be under neighborhood control, and does their work require professional expertise and training?

On the issue of where to locate authority, the answer seems clear from the kinds of crimes these men must handle: large-scale quasi-business "organized" crime; systematic refusal of large-scale land or factory owners to obey laws concerning adequate housing, adequate pollution control, and so on; embezzlement, tax evasion, and other white-collar crimes. These do not seem possible or appropriate to cope with on a neighborhood basis. Indeed, many such categories of crime are already dealt with on a Federal basis, and certainly metropolitan or even regional policing makes sense in these areas. The policemen involved would rarely if ever need to be "on the street" in any particular neighborhood, and their work would affect much wider areas—so wider areas should govern it.

But this issue of size leaves open the issue of professionalization. On the one hand, there is evidence in this realm of police work—from the growing use of large-scale private detective agencies, the growing importance of electronic detectors and computer analysis of financial accounts—that public police have not kept pace with the degree of technical expertise now required by much of the public. But on the other hand, there is the necessity of making sure that national, regional, or metropolitan police forces, too, as well as neighborhood peacekeepers, are kept under civilian control—a necessity not easily achieved, as the history of the FBI makes clear, and one that itself will require considerable social innovation. Whether there is any way to meet the requirement for technical skill while still preventing the emergence of a "professional" career subculture in this kind of police work is not clear, and will require further study.

In examining the possibilities, one factor should be kept in mind: de-careering the police and transforming them into a civilian institution can be seen not only as a step towards liberal democracy—that is, the establishment of the consent of the governed as the key to legitimate action by the government—but also as a step towards radical or participatory democracy—that is, blurring and ultimately dissolving the very line that separates the governed and the governors. If the latter were seen as the goal, then deprofessionalization of even the technical police, as well as the street police, would be important. If only the former is the goal, then there may be other ways to achieve the result of civilian control in spheres of police work where technical expertise remains important. In any case, in regard to street peacekeeping there seems no doubt that civilianization would advance both liberal and participatory democracy without damaging any necessary professional competence.

One thing is clear: the Black community has a special stake in establishing democratic control over the "technical police" in the broader community, as well as in the realm of neighborhood peacekeeping in its own streets. Whether metropolitan police do in fact enforce laws against large-scale owners of substandard housing, for example, is of key importance to the black community. In the absence of democratic control of the metropolitan "technical police," it is clear that the invisible powerful will prevent such enforcement. So whether de-careering the technical police is a workable road to democratic control or not, there needs to be careful study of what would be.

Model-building is not enough; we must also examine the politics of change towards one or another of these models of community control of the police.

The only city in which a sustained demand for neighborhood control along the lines of Model I has turned it into a serious political issue seems to be Washington, D.C. There the Black United Front has demanded neighborhood election of precinct police commissions—in the context of a series of homicides of civilians (almost all Black) by policemen (all white) and the killing of a white policeman by a Black civilian. The BUF demand was picked up by a group of Black businessmen, some Black clergymen, and a number of white and racially mixed groups in the city—such as the Democratic Central Committee, a Lawyers Committee made up of about 45 lawyers ranging from radical to moderately conservative, the local ADA chapter, and the Center for Emergency Support—a grouping of liberals and radicals who have acted as an energizing focus and research/education group on issues of institutional racism. In Washington, the demand has been politically strengthened by the lack of democratic legitimacy of the city government (which is appointed from the White House and heavily constrained by Southern Congressmen). In the total absence even of a fiction of city-wide democratic control over the police, the claims of neighborhood democracy have been strengthened. The strongest pressure has come from upsurges of rage from the Black community after each homicide of a Black civilian has been ruled "justifiable." Young white people have been uneasy about the police, and in the wake of the Chicago Democratic Convention, increased white support for new controls over the police became visible. Opposition to neighborhood control has come from the police, the white business community, the two large newspapers, and the Southern Congressmen who control the city's budget. Washington's city government has tried to appease both "law and order" and "community control" pressures by issuing slightly stronger restrictions on police use of guns, by calling for new advisory precinct boards, etc. Their efforts have had little effect.

Efforts in the direction of Model II have come almost entirely from Black or Spanish-speaking communities (perhaps in a few Appalachian white "ghettoes" like Uptown Chicago), with only momentary outside support from the Federal government or foundations.

The radical deprofessionalizing of some police roles, as in Model III, seems not to have become a political issue anywhere; but the splitting of police functions into several distinct roles and the recruitment of more "community" people (but no effort towards democratization of the command line) has been urged by the President's Crime Commission. A "community participation" (but not control) project in Washington, developed by outside agencies (the National Institute of Mental Health, especially) to test the Crime Commission's proposals, has triggered considerable enmity from neighborhood organizers on the ground that it will simply extend and intensify police control over the community (through informers, etc.), rather than the reverse.

Obviously, what political strategy is developed in achieving Black control over police in the Black community depends heavily on which model one intends to pursue, and which end result within them one hopes to achieve. Let us assume, however, that a decision is made to pursue a combination of Models I and III—which together seem to offer the fullest control over a police force to those in the neighborhood, by transforming both the formal lines of command and the informal interpersonal processes to converge on the community. The issue of police behavior (brutality, harassment, neglect) is sufficiently "hot" and the absence of democratic control so palpable even in cities that elect their mayor, that it would seem possible to mobilize more and more of the Black community in support of a Model I/III arrangement, through a sustained campaign. Then, when the level of demand is high and the refusal of the police and city government to change is clear, the Black community could probably—perhaps, but not necessarily, with the support of white liberals and radicals—move to establish a strong version of Model II.

Such a countervailing "community union to police the police" could then become not simply a grievance-processing organization, but also a continuous pressure group for the adoption of a Model I/III arrangement *in the form of a present ver-*

49

sion of what the future Model I/III control would look like. In other words, a strong community union to police the police could (1) itself put peacekeepers on the street—unarmed, distinctively uniformed, oriented to conflict resolution rather than Enforcing the Law, drawn from women, young dropouts, clergymen, and so on; (2) itself patrol the police, taking evidence of bad behavior and offering to settle problems instead of the police; (3) hear and investigate and judge complaints; (4) mobilize political pressure for the transfer of bad policemen, bad precinct commanders, and so forth; and (5) keep up constant pressure for the transfer of power over the neighborhood police to the neighborhood itself. It must be clear that such a community union to police the police would be a focus of intense political conflict, including great hostility and possibly physical danger from the police. But if the groundwork in organizing community support for a Model I/III arrangement had been well done, the very intensity of political conflict over a strong Model II might persuade the city to allow Model I/III to be established. In any case, it is hard to see how democratic civilian control over a staff of armed men who are widely believed to hold a monopoly over legitimate violence and who are well organized in a separate subculture and a strong political force can be re-established without intense political conflict.

7

The Three-Hundred-Years War

For more than three centuries, white America has been engaged in an unending war of conquest against the Blacks.* The general staff in that war has changed from generation to generation. But for most of the history of the war, working-class whites have been foot soldiers on the front line (taking the worst shelling, getting the least booty, and following the blindest orders). Middle-class whites have been sailors and airmen—firing from a distance with little sense of the consequences of their acts, usually staying reasonably protected from retaliation, and being allowed much more leave time. Most political and intellectual attention has been paid to the Black side of the war, but we believe the effects of the long war on the white draftees who fight it also demand attention and concern.

First, however, a brief review of the war itself: When it began, it was clearly warlike. It did not take the form of conquering land, as did the overlapping wars against Indian America and Mexican America. But the war against the Blacks did involve the capture at gunpoint of large numbers of the enemy, their transportation to concentration plantations, the destruction of their cultural identity, their use as slave labor. All three of these wars of conquest have in recent years grown much more subtle—so much so that it may seem extreme to say that relations between the races in America are in a permanent undeclared state of war. But the warlike origins of relations between white America and the Mexicans, the Indians, and the Blacks are still so important that there is a qualitative difference between those three cases on the one hand and relations between old WASP America and all the immigrant groups—Chinese,

* This paper was developed in long and fruitful discussions during 1969 among the members of the Center for Emergency Support, an anti-racist organizing group in Washington, D.C. In most ways it is a communal creation.

Irish, Polish, Italian, Jewish—on the other. The three defeated peoples are still treated as if they were under military occupation, and the war against them goes on in subtler ways. For example, if warfare is the use of organized massive killing against a population in order to control it and to benefit the victors, let us take just a look at two present aspects of American relations with the Blacks:

• Twice the proportion of Black babies as of other Americans die within their first year of life.

• Twice the proportion of young Black men as would be expected by random selection or according to their proportion of the American population are killed and wounded in the American War against Vietnam.

Naturally no one specifically chooses each of these Black children or young men to die; but the quiet war kills them. The social system constructed and ruled by white Americans arranges for them to die. If they were to live, more whites would have to die (in the swamps of Vietnam or the wards of American hospitals), unless the society radically changed its policies, its priorities, and perhaps its structure. So the warfare goes on, chronic and subtle and using weapons of money, prestige, and politics rather than weapons of steel—except when the Blacks turn to nonviolent or semiviolent disorder as a weapon of their own.

In the long and subtle war against the Blacks, we have suggested, the white middle class are airmen and sailors. We have also suggested that (like the troops in most wars of conquest) they have won some booty; but also like draftees in most wars, they have in addition suffered considerable restrictions on their own freedom. One side of the history of American race relations is the history of the efforts of the white middle class to move back and forth from seeking more booty to quitting the "army" to re-enlisting for more booty. The other side of that history is the effort of Black America to sally out against the siege that has surrounded them, each sally followed by a retreat or even a temporary surrender. The present racial crisis in

---

* The use of even more subtle means to control and subordinate women in American society suggests that ancient wars of slavery can be even more carefully refined than in the case of American racism.

America results from the determination of Black Americans to end the war, once and for all, on the basis of equality rather than surrender. That crisis finally puts the starkest possible question to the white middle class: are they more wedded to booty from the war, or to the freedom they might achieve for themselves if the war were over?

Before we talk about the benefits of freedom and an end to the war, we must face, acknowledge, and understand the fact that there has been booty for the troops. Only the most self-blinded liberal can deny that he benefits from the war against the Blacks—but there are such liberals, and they cannot even think of liberating themselves until they understand what they gain from the war. (But it should also be understood that the *big* booty goes, naturally enough, to the higher officers in the war—the general staff—and that is not the middle class. We will come back later to what that booty is.) What do middle-class whites gain from the war they and their fathers and their fathers' fathers have fought in, on and off, for so long?

Perhaps their gains can best be seen through concrete cases:

• Given some ceiling on the total number of 18-year-olds who can be admitted to college each year, a higher proportion of young whites is able to be admitted because a far lower proportion of young Blacks is "qualified." (That is, poverty established by white decisions on how to organize the economy, education aborted by the grade and high schools owned and managed by whites, and other such factors exclude Blacks under the standards set by the whites who own and manage the colleges.)

• The costs of "pleasant living" in suburbia are lower because large proportions of the Black population are prevented (by economic deprivation or racial exclusion) from competing for and pushing up the price of these amenities, and because tax money that might otherwise have been shared on expansive houses, grassy parks, new schools, and clean streets for the whole metropolitan area can be kept in great part for use in the white suburbs. (For example, given a ceiling on FHA loans for housing, the decision to not make such loans available in Black inner-city areas made more money available to help the white middle class buy suburban homes.)

• Middle-class white housewives who live near large concentrations of Black people have a much easier time finding and paying for maids and housekeepers because a large proportion of Black women are urgently required by poverty to take such jobs at low wages.

It should be noted that not a single one of these items of booty is dependent on personal feelings of racism held by the white soldiers. It is true that in moments of crisis, when the ordinary white troops are confronted with the reality of their booty and forced to square it with their own assumption that they are not at war with anybody, they *may* resort to personal racism to explain the situation. Indeed, they may then sound much more racist than their commanding officers—just as infantrymen slogging through the mud of Vietnam are much more likely to swear at "gooks" and "slants" than are the generals in the Pentagon. But these epithets are not essential to carrying on the war and are much less important to doing so than the institutions and the orders which send the troops to the jungle in the first place. Just as the white housewife, confronted with how she benefits from the quiet war in getting a maid, *may* respond that Black women enjoy menial work, that Blacks don't need much money because they don't understand or need very expensive consumer goods anyway (except "flashy" ones like Cadillacs which would not be good for them), that they can't do better jobs in any case, that they should be grateful for crumbs of charity, and so on. But these reactions are *not necessary*. They are fairly frequent among the infantry—the working-class whites—but in large parts of the middle class they are not considered respectable (although some middle-class whites have invented euphemisms, like "culturally deprived").

In many skirmishes, the white troops have no more contempt or hatred for the Black enemy than do the tired soldiery in any war. They explain their actions much more by custom, by "that's orders," by the unavailability or unlivability of alternatives than by anger directed at the other side. In the face of Black resistance, the white middle class feels both terribly threatened and deeply troubled—wracked with fear, filled with admiration, torn by guilt—anything but calm. It is clear why soldiers who think they may have their booty taken away from them might feel fear; the origins of guilt and especially of admiration must, however, be searched for in the other aspects of being a front-line soldier in the quiet war.

One such aspect is the difficulty the troops find in squaring the immediate orders of their commanding officers with the long-range moral proclamations of those same officers. The result is guilt—the reaction that many white soldiers in the War Against the Blacks recognize in themselves most clearly, and the one they have turned into occasional action. Guilt is a response to the deprivations of *others,* and to one's own complicity in those deprivations. In the white draftees, it stems from the difficulty of squaring traditional American moral rhetoric— which denies the decency and even the very existence of a war against Blacks—with the reality of that war. So guilt has fueled most of the traditional white support for civil-rights legislation. But even guilt is a limited response, an outward-looking rather than inward-looking one. And indeed the soldier is taught to look outward, at the wounds of others, rather than inward, at the less obvious wounds he suffers himself. For so long as he looks outward, he represents little threat to the military hierarchy in which he finds himself. If he looked inward, at his own losses, he would be far more dangerous to the general staff. Guilt may inhibit his hand against the Blacks, but only self-knowledge of self-interest can get him to raise his hand against the general staff.

It is indeed the inkling of a notion that he himself has suffered losses from the war that is most likely to trigger admiration, as against fear or guilt, in white troops who face the Blacks across a battle line. That seed of admiration for those who dared lift their hands against an occupying army can grow into the whites' own mutiny. That growth occurs when the whites awaken to a sense of their own deprivation.

What then are the white soldier's deprivations? Let us look at them as concretely as we did his booty:*

• In order to police the Blacks, he has to pay for the police. Thus most social workers, many metropolitan policemen, and

* As should be clear, "his" means either "his" or "her." The grammatical convention may be one of those subtle means of controlling women that is referred to above.

other similar occupations would literally not have to be paid for—the people could be doing other jobs—if urban Black populations were not kept poor, distraught, and troublesome.

• Even worse, the middle-class white must cramp and constrain himself into becoming a policeman. Thus the white teacher in a Black school is given orders to turn Black poor children into white middle-class grownups. To do this he must teach the children that the special dialect of English that they speak is not a language, but the corruption of a language; that the use of their intelligence to grapple with the real world they know is not intelligence, but a rejection of the great ideas of Western civilization; and so on. So he must break his students' spirit to teach them dead facts—and in the process he has to guard himself from responding warmly to them, their language, their intelligence. He has to surrender his own spontaneity, his own pleasure in learning and teaching, his own search or demand for enough resources to do a good job of teaching, in order to keep the Blacks subordinated. When he fails to make his students turn themselves inside out, he either blames them as "poor raw material" or himself as a "bad teacher." Even if he takes the third way out and becomes a rebel against the school system, he finds the contradictions between being white and trying to trigger Black self-confidence to be heart-rending. (The teacher's payoff for all this daily torment is that his own son has a better chance to enter college because he has taught his students so badly—but is the booty worth the price?)

• In the process of keeping Black people out of the suburbs, he keeps himself out of the city and has to travel hours every day to reach and leave his job. Thus the concomitant of the booty of FHA suburban loans is the ulcer, the crippling crash, the pollutionary lung cancer, and the highway tax bill that are created by the long auto ride. Nor, when he turns to mass transit, does he find his life transformed by subways; and he learns that so long as he insists on keeping racism, the cities are unbearable. Again, is the booty worth the price?

These specific abandonments of cash or liberty are, however, merely incidental to (or merely a part of) the major price the soldier pays for his booty: the *general habit of obedience*. Confronted by a troublesome subject people who must constantly be reconquered, the soldier reinforces his own commitment to his generals. Since his generals, when compared with the enemy, seem to be a heightened version of himself, he identifies with his officers and takes their word for the situation. He abandons the search for alternatives, new social processes, new institutions.

In 1968 there were several classic cases of the use of the War Against the Blacks to inculcate the habit of obedience in whites. In Wilmington, Delaware, after the murder of Dr. Martin Luther King and a small wave of attacks on property by some roving groups of Blacks, the Governor ordered the National Guard to patrol the city. It continued to do so for nine months, to the accompaniment of a drum fire of accusations against Black organizations. Although its presence cramped the liberties of whites as well, there was little outcry at militarization of the city. In New York City, union teachers opposed to the exercise of community control of the schools by Black communities like Ocean Hill-Brownsville lined up in support of supervisors whom they had previously opposed, when the issue of the war against the Blacks became intense. Facing an "enemy" across the trenches, they stopped mutinying against their own officers. The whole "law and order" cry of 1968 was another case: middle-class and working-class whites accepted —even demanded—restrictions of their own constitutional liberties—in order that these restrictions should apply (more rigorously) to Blacks.

The place of the attenuated racial war in several more general systems of obedience is hard to specify. But the process by which students are brought to accept versions of education that ignore or repress their feelings and ideas about the world, in order to "get ahead" in school or the job market; or the process by which labor unions are brought to surrender all insurgency on working conditions or business arrangements like the prices of products, keeping only wages as their area of conflict; or the process by which suburbanites are brought to accept unsafe cars and polluted air as an inevitable part of modern life— these processes seem close to the heart of the reason for the war against the Blacks. To the extent that people kick over these controls, they discover themselves *de facto* allies of the Blacks, in a mutiny against the white general staff; and to the extent that they have decided to become allies of the Blacks, they have found themselves forced to question and ultimately to revolt against the systems of order that have constrained them too. (Thus white parents, students, and teachers in New York who "crossed over" to support Black communities in the fight over community control found they had to break open the closed schools, resist principals and police, and redefine who should control the school system and the educational process; and white students, parents, and teachers who began from the other direction to rebel against the school authorities for their own reasons —like wanting an education—soon found they were *de facto* allies of the Black insurgents and had to redefine the nature of a good education for both whites and Blacks.)

Thus the "general staff" of the white war against Black America turns out to be the top leadership of most of the large-scale institutions of American life: large corporate business, large corporate-style government agencies, unions, the great educational and media machines, the military and police, the big-city political machines and their national parties.

Some of these leaders win direct payoffs from their conquests in the war itself—the ability to pay low wages to Black workers or charge high rents to Black families, the ability to gather huge and easily controlled voting majorities from Black populations, the ability to impress into military service large numbers of young Black men. But many of the white warlords who laid out and took command of one or another sector of the war chiefly in order to win certain booty from the Blacks have probably been finding that in the new ultra-industrial period since World War II, their payoffs from cheap Black labor are no longer as large and important as they once were. Now, and increasingly, they carry on the war for the secondary payoffs from the whites in the army of occupation: the payoff that issues of economic advantage and political power are obscured by the mere fact of the war, so that the chief function of the war is to call attention to itself; and the payoff in creation of the habit of white obedience.

If the war began to fuel more mutiny than obedience from whites, one of its major present payoffs would be called into question, and the general staff might well decide to abandon the war itself and seek other ways of reasserting its control of white lives.

For these reasons, then, it would seem that whites who have rediscovered certain needs of their own now thwarted by the existence or by the leadership of the war against the Blacks, and whites who have already decided that their moral commitments and loyalties are deeper to the Blacks they have been told to fight than to their "own" generals, should both focus on mutiny against the major warlord institutions as a way of achieving their ends. For the Wallace movement, which has defined much of its anger as a protest against rising taxes, rising prices, and frozen wages and small-business profits, this means defining the "enemy" not as the Blacks who are the most visible enemy, but as the social structure, institutions, and leadership that benefits from low wages, high prices, and high taxes on middling incomes. For the liberals who have defined their commitment as anti-racist, it means aiming against those same warlord institutions rather than trying to give direct aid to the Blacks or to make the war less cruel and foreign aid to the occupied territories more generous.

What does mutiny mean, under these circumstances? There has already begun to be some:

• White students have decided that their university's complicity in drafting them and refusal to let them develop new courses relevant to their needs is as destructive to them as its exclusion of Blacks and suppression of Black culture is to Blacks; so they have taken parallel action with the Blacks to win democratic control of such issues.

• White housewives have discovered that the same grocery chains that charge the poor more money for less fresh meat charge them more than would make a decent profit—and have decided that since high food prices are a threat to them too, they should boycott grocery chains till the prices come down.

• White professionals (very few, but a few) have discovered that large corporate farmers and chemical corporations not only drive poor Black farmers off the land but use DDT in such a way as to poison food, animals, and white professionals; so they have begun political campaigns against the DDT users.

59

• White liberals have discovered that police forces armed and trained to repress Black insurgency can do the same to white demonstrations; so they have started to probe for new ways to guarantee democratic control of the police.

• White homeowners and small businessmen have learned that superhighways aimed through Black neighborhoods destroy theirs too, and have organized to stop the oil-auto-highway lobby that demands more highways.

There are also many imaginable mutinies that have not yet even begun to happen:

• Nowhere have small "marginal" white businessmen who sell liquor, food, clothes to the Black communities decided that their real opponent is not the Blacks but the landlords, the banks, and the wholesalers whose rates are so high that bare profit-making dictates the high prices imposed upon the Blacks.

• Nowhere have the great proportion of white teachers in a large city decided that their own professional commitment to decent teaching requires the cracking of the educational administration.

• Nowhere have suburbanites decided to press for reconstruction of the metropolitan areas into clusters of centers where people live, work, and play—thus vastly decreasing the traffic volume, and lengthening their lives.

Enough such mutinies, and the general staff may decide to end the longest war in American history—or if it cannot or will not do so, may find itself toppling; too rigid and unbending in the storm. What would a North American society look like that was not structured around the War Against the Blacks?

• The Blacks would decide how to structure their own society. How? There will undoubtedly be serious debates: Integration—real integration, on a basis of equality rather than fitting into empty slots in a white society? A separate national territory? A federation of scattered Black neighborhoods into a continent-wide Black semi-nation? Close political, cultural, and economic connections with Africa? Two or more of these simultaneously?

• The present white authority structure would be badly damaged, if not destroyed—because so much of its legitimacy is attached to the habit of obedience learned in the War Against the Blacks, and because so much of that legitimacy would have been destroyed in the mutinies before the end of the war. How far would the new democracy extend, and what forms would it take? Would consumer pressure against chain stores and independent storekeepers' organizing against banks and wholesalers have created new popularly controlled credit unions, new consumer-owned coop stores and farms and factories? Would anti-highway protests move towards reconstruction of cities so that living, working, and having fun were integrally connected in new multi-purpose neighborhoods with their own democratic governments in control of police, schools, zoning, and so on? Would schools and universities have been redefined as places for anyone, regardless of social class or cultural background, to pursue his own best knowledge—using books and teachers as aids rather than determinants, in a free-flowing rather than a rigid way?

It is these *possibilities*—undoubtedly there are many others—that the War Against the Blacks now prevents. It is necessary to organize mutinies against that war if these possibilities are to be grasped and made real. Just as there are many arenas in which mutiny might take place, there are many forms of organization that might be pursued.

• Vocational groups with a single large employer might address the constraints imposed on them by their own institution's commitment to the war (for example, teachers vs. educational administrators, factory workers vs. large industrial corporations and union bureaucracies, civil servants vs. the great government agency heads).

• Neighborhood groups might address the institutions and problems of physical/social planning, policing, schooling, and so on that are now undemocratically controlled.

• Groups of free-floating communities that are only partly geographical in base—religious or ethnic communities, professionals without a single large employer, and so forth might develop a more free-wheeling, "guerrilla" politics of opposition to the old institutions of their community and creation of new versions of it. (Thus Jews for Urban Justice, vis-a-vis Jewish institutions; a Lawyers Committee, vis-à-vis legal institutions; storekeepers vis-à-vis banks and wholesalers; and so on.)

In any of these arenas, the organizing group should see itself

61

as much as possible as a miniature of what that arena should look like after the War Against the Blacks is over. In that way, it is both an example to others and, as it grows, itself a chunk of the future society. For these reasons, two processes are important for organizing clusters:

First, it is important that they build into their organizing a commitment to the world outside their vocation, their neighborhood, or their community. Otherwise, their insurgency can take the form of a fighting, but only self-protective, guild or enclave. (Ideally, this should mean that organizations of teachers have built-in requirements for checking with parents and students; organizations of social workers, with groups of welfare recipients; and so on.)

Secondly, as soon as possible the members ought to commit themselves to contributions of serious amounts of money and work-time to the joint effort. (This may seem obvious, but the conventional arrangement is for civic or political groups to raise enough money—often from outside—to hire an "organizer" and rely on little work or involvement by members except in "meetings" to decide "policy.")

There is an old piece of rabbinical wisdom: "If we are not for ourselves, who will be? If we are for ourselves only, what are we? If not now, when?" There can be no sharper political tool for ending the War Against the Blacks. If whites do not mutiny against their own oppression, no one else will; if they oppose *only* their own oppression, they will not end it and will only make their foxholes in the War a little snugger—temporarily. It is both questions that must be answered: *If not now, when?*

Part II: White Transformation:
From Last-Gasp Liberal to Political Guerrilla

8
The Minority Mandate

Two mandates were handed down in the 1964 election—one by 61 % of the American voters; the other by 39 % of the voters.* The first seems obvious, even overwhelming; but an understanding of the second may be even more crucial in moulding a decent future for American society.

The first mandate was voiced by the 61 % of our people who voted for President Johnson, and the sizable majority who voted to keep a large number of liberal Democrats in the Senate and send a large number to the House of Representatives. The claim is made that this was a mandate from the people who were for things, for the twentieth century. But that 61% of the country encompassed so many different versions and dreams of the twentieth century that it is easier to say what they were against than what they were for. There are few common hues among voters whose political spectrum ranges from Henry Ford's modern corporatist vision and North Carolina's business-managed token desegregation to the gray flannel welfarism of Joseph Tydings in Maryland, and still further, to the black-and-white-together Populism of the Mississippi Freedom Democrats and the desperate demand for an entire reshaping of the city that wells up out of Harlem; from the quasi-rational bookkeeping with H-bombs by Robert McNamara's computers to the vigorous demands for world-wide disarmament on the banners of the National Committee for a SANE Nuclear Policy, and still further to the Gandhian pacifism of Bayard Rustin.

The mandate was against turning control of nuclear weapons over to generals in the fields; it was against increasing the military budget and re-igniting the arms race; it was against using H-bombs in Vietnam; it was against letting Mississippi and Ala-

* This article was written after the 1964 election but before Lyndon Johnson's massive escalation of the War Against Vietnam.

65

bama put the Negroes back "in their place"; it was against filling our streets with policemen who could arrest on suspicion and convict with the third degree; it was against selling TVA; it was against making Social Security voluntary. In short, it was against abolishing the world—literally, with H-bombs—and against abolishing the United States government—figuratively, with Congressional legislation. But it certainly was no single mandate for what the world or the United States government should look like. It was not even a clear mandate for change. The mandate for change came from elsewhere.

The significance is not simply that the 39 % of our people who voted for Senator Goldwater wanted drastic changes made —though they did. Much more important, the fact that 39 % of our people voted for him and his program is a clear warning and a firm mandate that changes must be made—though not the kinds of changes the 39 % wanted. For when almost two-fifths of the people say that they detest the society they are living in so deeply that they would rather dismantle its government, and take a chance on blowing up the world, than keep on living the way they have been—then something is wrong with that society.

If 39 % of our people are howling protests or muttering in anger, they should be listened to. They are not entitled to be obeyed, nor to have their programs adopted. But we owe it to them and to ourselves to see if their protests and their anger could be eased or erased by taking steps, not to abolish the world, but to transform it; not to tear the government in Washington apart, but to reshape it. And it is in that sense that we should take our most important mandate from the election to be the mandate of the minority: to make the changes that are needed if American society is to become a decent place to live in, a decent enough place for the 39 % to want to live in.

The basic question is why they were willing to take a chance on dying rather than to keep on living in the America we have. The reason is that the American people now stand at the edge of a deep but narrow precipice. On the other side lies a society of economic abundance, in which "work" is no longer laborious and in which large numbers of people may hold new kinds of paid "jobs" that are now merely amateur avocations, such as

66

those of "student," "politician," "grandmother," and "civil rights worker." It might be the kind of society in which everyone—not just professors—would be entitled to a paid sabbatical every seventh year; or in which we might even decide to give people a free income, the way we decided in 1862 to give people free land, just because they are people.

This society also will be a society of world community at some level, a society in which we might have total disarmament with international inspection and enforcement as nations continue to pursue their own political and economic goals by all means other than war or the threat of war—or in which we might even have a full-scale world government.

This society will be one of an increasing share in political decisions by every human being; a society in which the dispossessed of Mississippi—Black and white—take a hand in deciding their own destiny; a society in which such new forms of political expression as the sit-in become as legitimate as free speech, and new forms of neighborhood government are invented, in which perhaps workers have a greater control of the organization in which they work (again like professors, who help decide the future of the university); in which even students may come to be accepted as a legitimate element in the real government of their schools.

Now those three major aspects of the new society across the precipice—the abundance that leads to leisure and to new kinds of work; the extension of political community to the whole world; and the deepening and broadening of a share in democracy for people who have up till now not had much chance to guide their own destinies—frighten some people. There are some who could not bear to live in a world where the Negroes won't stay in their place—which is down there—the Russians and Chinese won't stay in their place—which is far away over there—and the politically excluded and dispossessed won't stay in their place—which is somewhere around, but invisible. There are some people who could not bear to live in the new society; but it seems unlikely, if we look around, that there are so many of these people as to make up 39 % of our country. They do make up the radical right, but that is much smaller than 39 %. The real

67

question is why the Radical right gets enough support to put together 39% of the vote behind a candidate that shares much of its program.

The answer is that American society has been standing too long on the edge of the precipice, horrified by the depths and fearful of the jump to the new world. Some of our people have grown dizzy with fear and frustration. They might not mind jumping, but they do mind standing. Therein lies the danger, and the warning, of the second mandate. For what 39 % have said is that they are sick unto death of standing still, they would rather hurtle into the depths than stand any longer at the edge. And that means we must gather our strength and energy, and leap the precipice into the new world. If we stand still any longer, the proportion who would rather fall than stand is likely to grow—the 39 % of this year may be 45 or 50 % by 1968.

Let us look beyond metaphor, to the concrete issues. We have been "standing still too long at the edge of the precipice" in the sense that from 1938, when Congress passed the Fair Labor Standards Act, to 1964, when it passed the Civil Rights Act, there was no major legislative step towards social reform. From 1940, when the River Rouge strike won unionization of the Ford auto plants, to 1963, when Birmingham signalled the national upheaval of the civil rights movement, there was no broad political action involving large numbers of Americans.

Let us look at the problems that so overwhelmed 39 % of our people as to drive them into the arms of the right wing. They said there was too much violence in the streets. Indeed there is— but it must be cured at the roots, not smashed by police action. And curing at the roots means ending the joblessness that has now reached 15 % among urban youth; it means ending the senselessness and absurdity of the city, ending the powerlessness of the slumdweller and his suburban cousin, who both feel "You can't fight City Hall." In short, ending the violence in the streets means both reconstructing the economy and reconstructing the cities—not just the buildings, but the urban social system.

At the Federal level, it means working out ways of encouraging the new jobs—the only jobs that can't be automated—the jobs that mean dealing with people and ideas, not goods and paper—the jobs of poetry and politics.

How do we use the tax system—not, as we do now through depreciation allowances, to encourage the replacement of an "old" automated factory with a new, still more automated factory—but instead to encourage people to give small and middle-sized contributions to Congressional election campaigns, to CORE and SNCC, to SANE and to Young Americans for Freedom and to Parents and Taxpayers in New York? In short, we could encourage the new and vital forms of political action, of whatever program and bent, that are trying to energize the fearful, the frustrated, the angry, and the hopeless. For the new vocation of "political activator" is at least as important to the country as those of teacher, scientist, and social worker, for whose encouragement we set up rules for making contributions tax-deductible.

How do we use the Federal public works program—that is, deliberate Federal deficits—to pay not only for billion-volt, billion-dollar nuclear accelerators but also for hundreds of live theaters where real people get paid well to be actors, for thousands of nursery centers where grandmothers whose grandchildren live a thousand miles away can play grandma to a dozen neighborhood children and get paid a decent salary for it, for the education of slum kids to fill our empty, impersonal hospitals with nurses and aides who care about the patients?

Thinking about the local level also is important, because that 39 % also was right when it said too much authority over too many details was being taken by Washington. On the local level, ending violence in the streets means advancing local neighborhood action groups like The Woodlawn Organization in Chicago; it means turning New York City's paper schemes for neighborhood governments with "little city councils" and "little city halls" into reality; it means encouraging outfits like New York's Mobilization for Youth to join in rent strikes and sit-ins, instead of reprimanding them for doing so.

Or let us take another issue raised by the mandate of the 39 %. They said we have a "no win" foreign policy. They were right—but their solution was wrong when they said we should spend even more on weaponry. We will continue to have a no-win foreign policy so long as military victories are the primary goal. Certainly we win no victories for liberty in Vietnam, when every "victory" is conditioned on burning another peasant village or administering the water torture to another peasant boy. We can win no victories for liberty when every act is inhibited by fear that ours and others' H-bombs will explode, so that we take few chances on behalf of liberty.

Only in a world moving towards disarmament can we win real victories for liberty. Only in a world moving towards disarmament can we help topple the South African dictatorship with a democratic revolution before the Communists do it with a totalitarian revolution. Only in a world moving towards disarmament can we encourage dissent in Eastern Europe without risking world war. Only in a world moving towards disarmament could we use effectively what might be called the Unarmed Services of the United States—an Air Transport Force to assist underdeveloped nations without a rail or road network; a Disaster Corps like the old Seabees who could rebuild whole cities after earthquake or typhoon; a Conservation Corps for reforesting and irrigating the Sahara. These would be effective ways of winning victories for liberty—and they are the kinds of institutions we will need in the society that lies across the precipice.

But we must begin now. Another four years of stagnation, and we may well be too paralyzed with fear and frustration to move.

What did the mandate of 1964 mean in terms of immediate action? First, the American party system is undergoing a shakeup of the kind it has suffered only three times before—when the Federalist Party disappeared, when the Whigs transmuted themselves into Republicans, and when both Democrats and Republicans were thrown into disarray by the emergence of the Populist Party. The real question is, which of those three patterns will be the one that emerges? Will the Republican Party become so out of touch with the nation's needs that it dwindles away and lets all our important political debates take place within the Democratic Party, until the Democrats split over some future issues as John Quincy Adams and Andrew Jackson split the party? Or will the Republicans submerge as the Whigs did, build some new alliances, and emerge in some new guise, with a partially new program and approach? Or will the eruption of frustration and hostility that captured the Republican Party in 1964 subside as did the Populists, leaving both parties to reappear in their old form, with merely a more modern look?

No prediction can be certain of fulfillment, but there are reasons to believe that the Republican Party has gone too far and lost too much ever to become again the kind of party it was in the '40s and '50s. For decades the party could be described as a continuously renewed deal between little business and Eastern Established big business. The Establishment sold an anti-government ideology to the little businessman, in the hope that the little businessman would then keep the public government in Washington under control. That would leave the Establishment free to run its own private government without interference from Washington. The little businessmen bought the anti-government ideology in order to make sense, instead of despair, out of their own helplessness in the complexity of mid-century metropolitan society. Then, after adding moral fervor and indignation to the anti-government ideology, they sold it back to the Establishment for use as a rationalization and justification of the Establishment's insistence on private instead of public government. But now both sides are moving in their own separate directions: the Establishment is more and more closely tied to the government in Washington, while the little businessmen are taking the anti-government ideology so seriously that most of the Establishment is frightened and wants to switch over to the Democrats, in order to manage Washington in another fashion.

Many important Eastern Republicans "switched over" in action, if not in rhetoric, when they joined the Kennedy "coalition government." Douglas Dillon, McGeorge Bundy, Robert McNamara, John McCone, and dozens of lesser men actually moved into a Democratic administration. Now, at the grass roots, many Republicans who agree with these men have voted Democratic. The men in between—the party organizers, the small office holders—will tell the tale. It may well be that one reason these men were so paralyzed that they could not defend the party against the right-wing takeover was that, mentally, they had already more than half migrated to the Decorats. If they cannot muster the energy and commitment to take back the party now,

71

it will become wholly a vehicle for the frustrated and fearful Americans.

If the Republicans do become a right-wing party, we will go through a peculiar period in which effective American politics takes place only within the Democratic Party. It should be noted that insurgent groups—the Negroes, the peace movement, possibly the unemployed—may well be uncomfortable with a "bipartisanized" Democratic Party. They may try to break out of it, but will be fearful of doing so, as long as one-third of the country remains organized behind right-wingers in the revamped Republican Party.

In such a situation, almost everything might depend on the President. He has a large majority in the Congress—a majority large enough to expel some of the furthest right-wing Southern "Democrats" from the party caucus, and to pass a great deal of legislation that looks to the society on the other side of the precipice: full employment in new kinds of jobs, racial equality, major arms reductions and important steps towards a detente with both Russia and China. He could lead this majority *if he wants to.* Or, he could revert to the politics he played as Majority Leader of the Senate: always delaying before acting, and shifting position according to the immediate pressures but never more than necessary. In short, the politics of "Wait."

If the President moved forward quickly, he would probably end the frustration that produces such widespread support for right-wing ideology. If jobs were provided, street violence in the cities would drop, fears of Negro competition for scarce jobs would diminish; if integration moved ahead quickly, suburbanites would soon learn that property values do not drop; if sizable disarmament took place, the country would discover we were far less likely to suffer attack; if an active program of winning unarmed victories for liberty began, we would learn that we need not suffer the guilt and frustrations of trying to win liberty through torture, as in Vietnam. Thus the newly right-wing Republican Party would evaporate, and the Democratic Party would probably soon split up as the Jeffersonians did when new issues emerged.

On the other hand, a passive policy of no forward movement, no action to anger the Establishment or anyone else, would leave

American society standing still, with at least a third of our people frustrated and terrified. In that case, one can imagine widespread on-the-streets harassment of liberals (as in California, with night telephone calls and bomb threats, or in Mississippi, with night-riders.) The result probably would be a major increase in right-wing strength by 1968.

But must we leave this decision to the President? Must we depend wholly on him? There is every reason not to depend on him if we can avoid it. He may make the wrong decision; even if he wants to make the right one, he will probably need help from active and organized people who are running interference for him. Democracies do not survive as democracies by "trusting" Presidents to do their job for them. If we believe it necessary to move forward, we must use what means are available to us.

Vigorous concerted action must be taken in the Democratic primaries of 1966 and 1968 to defeat "moderate," conservative, or machine Democrats; to nominate principled and able liberals, militant Negroes, peace candidates who can pull part of the old Republican vote for the House and Senate. This requires local coalitions between people who care about poverty and unemployment, people who care about racial justice, people who care about improving the quality of our schools and cities, and people who care about moving toward world peace and disarmament.

Such local coalitions would not be easy to put together and keep together. They would have to include labor unionists, senior citizens, former peace Republicans, groups of the unemployed, mothers on welfare, militant Negro rent strikers and school boycotters, activist college students, professors and lawyers in reform politics, suburban housewives who care about peace and good schools—a mixed bag of different kinds of people. But such local coalitions would be necessary if the best of the new Democrats that have just appeared in the House of Representatives are to be kept there, and if hacks among the Senators and Congressmen are to be replaced. Such local coalitions would need help—ideas, money, prestige—from a similar national coalition; and they would need a program built around the large-scale reconversion of military effort into ending poverty in America and improving the quality of American life among the affluent.

73

(One other lever is available to at least some of the insurgents. That is an expansion and deepening of the politics of "creative disorder"—the politics of sit-ins, freedom votes, and rent strikes. Here there are two crucial questions: Can the Negroes, who began the recent wave of creative disorder, carry it into the Northern ghettoes in some form that will excite and involve Negro youth and that would also be seen by most northern whites as reasonably legitimate, even if militant? [Only if such new forms of creative disorder can be invented and accepted is there likely to be an avoidance of more riots that would tend to energize right-wing opposition.] Can poor and unemployed whites organize non-violent street action similar to that of the Negroes? Since the labor unions are the only "middle-class poor" analogous to the middle-class Negroes who got the sit-ins started, such a movement of the unemployed would need vigorous support from organized labor. So far the unions have not put forth the necessary effort.)

The program and the political procedures that have been outlined here would carry out both the majority and minority mandates that were handed down by our electorate in 1964. The program looks toward the sane use of our abundance to build a society of high quality and to wipe out poverty (and thus to end the violence that grows from poverty and alienation). It is a program for ending war and advancing liberty in the world (and thus for moving forward out of the "no win" foreign policy). It is a program for sharing real political power with all those who are presently excluded from it.

As for the political procedure, it is built chiefly on a coalition between the different groups that want to move forward each in its own way—a coalition built on the belief that none of them can move forward unless the others do, too. It also involves the acceptance of the new kinds of politics, the techniques of creative disorder, that are being invented by the groups that demand a new voice in deciding their own futures. Together, these new styles for, and new contents of, American politics would make it possible for us to leap the precipice and enter the new society.

There is only one thing to add. We have been talking about a presidential election, and presidential politics. That is an index to the historic fascination of Americans with the Presidency and its power, especially its power for bringing about progress. But good presidential politics is not simply whatever happens to come from "great" Presidents. It is democratic politics that makes men who may or may not be great into great Presidents. It is up to us.

9
The New Vocation: Activator

Young Americans are inventing a new and newly significant vocation. It is the vocation of politically activating the politically inert and the politically excluded.

The new vocation is being carried on in African villages, Mississippi cotton fields, Chicago suburbs, Harlem slums, Cleveland tenements, Kentucky mining towns. Some aspects of it are well known to the public—the work of the Peace Corps in teaching African villagers how to organize themselves both to build an irrigation system and to get attention from a bored and distant government; the work of SNCC, the Student Nonviolent Coordinating Committee, in encouraging Mississippi sharecroppers to demand a share in voting and in making all the other decisions that govern their future; and the work of the Northern Student Movement in tutoring Northern Negro slum children in the elements both of algebra and of the rent strike.

There are, however, other aspects of the new vocation that have so far received much less attention. Among these are the efforts of Students for a Democratic Society, a national organization of liberal and radical young people. Some SDS members work full-time on bare subsistence pay to help activate the urban poor. In Cleveland, for example, SDS is working with mothers who receive public welfare checks. SDS is encouraging them to think of themselves as citizens entitled to have a say in how large the welfare checks are and what they may be spent for, rather than as serfs who must be grateful for every crumb. Again, there are the efforts of students working for Turn Toward Peace to energize suburban businessmen who may be involved in domestic politics but who are apathetic about military strategy and world affairs. Many of these businessmen feel that foreign policy is too "foreign" and too much the experts' problem for them to get involved in, and they are therefore politically inert about such questions as world disarmament. But the Turn Toward Peace activators encourage them to see that even if they are in civilian businesses, their pocketbooks are affected by such issues as disarmament. Furthermore, Turn Toward Peace shows them that information on disarmament is publicly available—not "secret" or "too complicated to understand"—and that business-men therefore both can and should help make political decisions about disarmament.

There are many other such groups scattered around the country and the world. Most have received little public attention. But what has received least attention of all is that the Peace Corps and SNCC, as well as the other new forms of political activation, presage a new kind of career, that they are not simply isolated vacations from real life to be taken by a few of the young, but the seeds of a whole new kind of career.

Perhaps the first hesitant recognition that the elements of this growing phenomenon are not isolated but interrelated came when the Eleanor Roosevelt Foundation offered fellowships to some returning Peace Corps volunteers to enable them to work in the American civil rights movement. But the foundation itself regarded this only as a temporary measure, and was not en-visioning a career in which an activator might spend two years in Nigeria, three or four in Mississippi, another year working among migrant agricultural workers in California, and then some time among the hopeless men who have left the ghost mines of West Virginia to enter the ghost factories of Cleveland or Baltimore.

It is not, of course, inevitable that a full-fledged new career will emerge from the scraps and patches of the new vocation that now exist. Yet there are reasons to believe that American society is ready to create and support such a new career. For one thing, the very wealth of America is tending to bring it into being. At one level of our society, this wealth is making the vocation of political activation possible. In a poorer society, students are supported by the few families that can afford such luxuries (or by the state) only so long as they stay in school— or else they have to work part-time in farm, factory, or office, merely in order to support themselves. In America they can leave school and still have, or be able to find, reserves of money or support with which to pay for their subsistence while they activate the ghettos or the cotton fields. At another level, the very abundance of America is creating large reservoirs of people for whom none of the traditional jobs are available: those, on the increase now, who grow to eighteen or twenty to find that the jobs they expected have been automated out of existence; those of forty or fifty, somewhat fewer, whose jobs have been automated out from under them; those of sixty-five or seventy-five, the largest of the three groups, who would have died at fifty in a poorer society but who in America live long beyond retirement from their jobs. In their anger or puzzlement, these three new reservoirs of the jobless are ripe for political action, and a few of the people among them have already found that one job for which they need little training is the job of political activation. Thus both affluent Americans and poverty-stricken Americans increasingly see the possibility of a career in political activation as the way ahead—or as the way up.

There are also pressures from the world at large that will tend to encourage the building of the new vocation in America. The shifts from a military to a political focus in world policy, and from Europe and the Soviet Union to the Southern Hemisphere, will probably mean an increased demand for political activators. For as these shifts occur, the Cold War more and more clearly changes into a complex and confusing series of political and economic conflicts over the ways in which various parts of the underdeveloped world will develop. Since in the underdeveloped world the activation of the politically inert is probably a prerequisite to any serious political and economic progress, many new activators will be needed. For these reasons, the American response to the new situation may well be the strengthening of the present Peace Corps and the creation of similar organizations to carry on political activation in the underdeveloped world. Perhaps we can even imagine the creation of a sort of International SNCC for South Africa, intended to help build a democratic base for a democratic revolution there. But even short of this ultimate possibility, there are likely to be many more opportunities for political activation overseas—and therefore a much greater likelihood that the new vocation will develop into a career at home.

If the emergence of the new vocation is to be encouraged, its present young practitioners need public recognition, respect, and money. Today some elements of the new vocation get direct support from government (as the Peace Corps); others (such as SNCC) depend chiefly on the churches and other "conscience" institutions in affluent parts of American society; still others (such as Students for a Democratic Society in their work with the urban poor) look especially to labor unions and foundations for help, but also draw on the money they themselves can earn in part-time jobs and on help from their liberal friends on faculties, and from some of their parents. (Many parents, however, are dubious about the new, unorthodox vocation. What kind of job is it, they ask, for an M.A. in economics—working in the slums at $15 a week?)

Some of the organizations that are working in the new vocation are tax-exempt under the rubric of education, and many of them have won support from some of the smaller foundations. (The Big Three—Ford, Rockefeller, and Carnegie—have steered shy of the new vocation.) But there is a basic political problem involved in raising money—not just a financial or a legal one. Activation of the politically excluded or apathetic is bound to shake the political status quo. When SNCC shakes an applecart in Mississippi it can count on help from Cleveland. But when SDS shakes an applecart in Cleveland, it is unlikely to get help there—and not very likely to get it from Mississippi. As the process of activation disturbs groups that are closer and closer to the centers of affluence and power in the United States —rather than at the fringes like Mississippi—the sources of both financial and psychological support are likely to dry up. Thus, when SDS encouraged groups in Cleveland and Baltimore to attack the local plans for the "war on poverty" because they left the poor out of the decision-making process, many respectable people who might in theory have supported the SDS approach were outraged that their own well-meaning plans should be criticized. When some young activators in the federally and municipally supported Mobilization for Youth in New York City undertook to lead rent strikes in Harlem, the lashback led to charges of subversion and threats to cut off support unless Mobilization acted less vigorously. Most of these threats came

79

from the city government; Federal officials like Attorney General Nicholas Katzenbach had fewer ties to local landlords who had been threatened by the rent strikes, and Katzenbach was therefore able to come to the defense of the "activators" in Mobilization. But the effectiveness of the activators was considerably reduced.

It is hard, therefore, to imagine that local sources of support can, over the long run, be of much help to local units of political activators. It is equally hard to imagine that Federal grants and Federal protection would continue to be available for long if political activators were helping excluded groups to keep on making trouble for powerful groups in New York, Mississippi, and Chicago. Somehow a kind of national "transfer payment system" might have to be arranged, with those among the affluent Americans in one area who were most committed to activation arranging to send money for, write articles and letters about, and generally give help to activators who were upsetting their opposite numbers somewhere else. Traditionally, the institutions most likely to take on such a thankless task are the foundations, the churches, and perhaps the labor unions, and the individuals most likely to help are the scholars. Funds would have to be made available to provide for a substantial number of one- or two-year grants at about subsistence level for students who wish to leave formal academic training to help activate the politically excluded. Colleges and universities could assist by granting course credit for the educational experience involved. Society at large could help by ending the military draft, which now keeps many young men so unsettled about their careers, or so fearful of losing a student deferment, that they cling to school and avoid any unusual departures from the regular pattern of life. And the kinds of social approval now given to the Peace Corps and, less warmly, to VISTA (the domestic peace corps) could be extended to these unofficial activators who wanted to rock the boat as tutors in Northern city slums, as voter registration agents in the Mississippi Delta, perhaps even as workers in countries (for example, South Africa) where the official Peace Corps cannot or will not go.

In addition, financial and social support should be made available to noncollegiate youth of about the same age range.

These youths, coming mainly from the excluded populations, could also act as political activators, but they would need another kind of program. They would not need to be trained in dealing with the politically excluded—they would know life in the slums all too well—but they would need to step back a pace from their own experience to see where and how it fits into a larger understanding of society. They must be given the opportunity, therefore, to attend special institutes and work projects directed by academically trained persons who are interested in the problems of political exclusion and specially trained for working with young people from the slums and backwaters of America.

Those of the excluded who had become newly active could thus gain access to the ideas developed by scholars and thinkers about the nature of their society, at the same time as they educated the academicians in the nature of social life among the politically excluded. In short, the emphasis at this age level in the new vocation should be upon the interchange of ideas: bringing together from both directions the stored knowledge of the university student and the active information of the previously excluded youth who has just become politically involved. The rich can learn from the poor, as well as vice versa.

Unfortunately, there are no easy ways to guarantee that political activators will continue in the new vocation instead of transferring into more traditional occupations. The attractions from the old vocations would be respectability, money, and relaxation from psychological pressures. Presumably the new vocation—as an abstract concept or idea—would gradually become more respectable as it became more firmly established. But in particular cases, stirring up the inert and excluded would probably seem to be highly provocative—and its practitioners would, at least locally and temporarily, seem disreputable. Only people who could stand up under local scorn would be likely to stay in the new vocation.

There will also be a tendency for many to move from political activation itself (in the form of direct involvement in the life of the dispossessed) into bureaucratic staffing of the agencies that have been necessitated by the new vocation. It is at this juncture that a union headquarters, an urban renewal agency, the Peace

Corps, and so on, would recruit people with field experience to move into desk jobs and paperwork. Some of this kind of movement is natural and makes good sense; but most of those in the new vocation should not leave it in this fashion. What is the alternative?

One of the major needs of the new vocation will be for older men of wisdom and experience to train new entrants into the field, while they themselves remain directly involved. Thus a number of the political activators at this age level would become "professors" of the new discipline, in the ancient sense that they would continue to "profess" the vocation themselves while teaching others to enter it. Thus, for example, someone in his forties who had been working in the Mississippi Delta might spend one year at a large university and then either return to the Delta or perhaps become a "professor" in a city slum such as Harlem.

Finally, much might be done to encourage older people to devote themselves to the new vocation after retiring from their conventional occupations. Indeed, these new recruits would be specially qualified to deal with communities of the aged who were on the verge of surrendering their previous political involvement in order to "join" the excluded. Older persons just joining the new vocation would be in the best position to reverse this trend and shift the aged into the area of political concern and commitment.

Looking down the career line that emerges from this sketch, it seems possible that the activator career would be best expressed through the establishment of many institute-workshops, kept deliberately small and equipped to accommodate people of all ages. Each of these might consist of twenty-five to fifty people (with one or two instructor-activators for every eight to ten student-activators), and contain new recruits, regular workers, and "professors." This network of "schools" would be analogous to the more traditional academic system; but its component parts would be much smaller and would be kept free of red tape. Each institute-workshop might be set up in conjunction with a particular action group, such as a labor union, CORE chapter, or public housing association. Support for these institutes as such would be useful, but the purpose of political activation would probably be best served by encouraging individual autonomy, through giving grants to individuals to go wherever they felt the worst deprivations of human rights and political involvement existed.

It must be emphasized that such grants could not do the whole job of bringing the new career into existence; but they could encourage its growth by providing for aid at the "critical points." If the vocation were to grow, of course, there would not only have to be money to pay its practitioners but there would have to be the kinds of practitioners who could bring *élan* and excitement to a drab life among worn-out people, practitioners who would be able to come back roaring with energy after a rent strike had collapsed or a group of suburban mothers had called them Communists.

In the long run, the activators could be successful only if their financial, psychological, and political support began to come not from those who were already affluent or already powerful, but from those most directly affected by the new vocation: from Negroes in Mississippi, mothers on welfare in Cleveland, businessmen in Chicago who became interested in disarmament, suburban mothers who create a center for consumer information. As these groups become politically active, they are more likely to support their own and others' activators, and if their political action brings results they are more likely to have the money and energy and knowledge with which to do the job. In this way, an investment in the new vocation would be likely to multiply the vocation's own support; and a constantly increasing proportion of Americans might find themselves involved in the new kind of work.

Of course, the new vocation would not be wholly new and utterly unprecedented. The idea that people should be paid for carrying on political action goes back to Athens, where the citizens were paid for casting their ballots and where, indeed, many of the citizens treated political activity as their chief concern and occupation. What would be new would be the great numbers of people who could spend their time in politics. For although politics has always been the main occupation of some human beings, to the extent that only a very few have held this human right, it has operated as the antithesis of a right, as if it were the acme of special and tyrannical privilege. It was

Aristotle who wrote that slaves would always be necessary if some men were to be free to think—until and unless, he added sardonically, the shuttles were to learn to weave without workmen. But what to Aristotle was a sarcastic aside has in the age of automation become living reality. In rich America, a great proportion of the population could make political activation its vocation. Then, if man is, as Aristotle said, the political animal, all men could for the first time afford to become fully human.

Indeed, as American society changes, the new vocation might become not only valuable but necessary. For the very richness of America is wiping out almost every traditional vocation. Most production jobs and many services are being automated out of existence. Cybernation is replacing the traditional jobs, leaving as work only those jobs that deal with human beings and values: poetry and politics. Our society must therefore accept work concerned with values as a legitimate vocational field—perhaps the only significant vocational field for the future. Otherwise, it will be unable to cope with the shift of almost the entire population out of the old areas of "employment," and most people will be forced into unemployment, hunger, and despair. If this happens, the remainder will be moved into overwhelmingly hard work, merely to keep the society going without violence or collapse—perhaps leading eventually to the use of police-state politics to keep the desperate under control.

In short, we face a crisis, the outgrowth of which will be either acceptance of political activation and democratic involvement for all—and as a paying job for vast numbers—or the acceptance of a politics in which half the society is revolutionary and the other half is tyrannical. If public understanding, acceptance, and support of the new vocation are forthcoming, then the road will be open to encourage a humane, decent, and democratic resolution of the crisis of baffling abundance.

10
The New Student Movement

In the last few months, especially since the war in Vietnam and protests against it have both escalated, a number of commentators from many wings of opinion—right, center, and socialist—have expressed a great deal of doubt about and disapproval of developments within the student movement. Most of these commentators have been from an older generation of American political activity. For what it is worth, it may be useful to compare their perceptions with the perceptions of someone whose basic political ideas were formed before, but only slightly before, the student movement received its great impetus from the 1960 sit-ins.

The students are making by no means a rigidly or vulgarly Marxist "class" analysis in the sheerly economic sense, but are more interested in all the "left-outs" rather than in just the economic "have-nots"—those who have been kicked off the bottom rungs of "status" and "power" ladders as well as those on the bottom rungs of the "class" ladder. They think of themselves as left-outs even though they come from affluent families. And their reaction is that no one ought to be "left-out"—that all human beings belong in the polis—that it is an outrage for *anyone* to be napalmed, starved, ignored, or segregated.

They analyze the reasons for the present exclusion of some people from the *polis* as partly the wish of the Establishment to make more money, but partly its grasp for power aside from wealth and partly a kind of disease that comes from focusing upon the machine the Establishment thinks it is running rather than upon the people who are really being run ragged. As the students see it, this disease involves the love of order, because the machine must run smoothly; anger at those who create disorder (though sometimes a willingness to buy order back at the price of placating the disorderly); and a willingness to treat people who do not fit the orderly assumptions as if they were not part of society at all.

For these reasons, the students believe that "the revolution" of which they speak must not only include a redistribution of wealth and the grasping of a share in power by those who presently have no power at all and the acceptance of all as entitled to human dignity, but also the reconstruction of society so that it does not act *or seem like* a machine, but *is* always and always *looks* like people. This is the real hope and meaning behind the slogans of "participatory democracy," "decentralization," "university reform," "the Third World," and so on. Otherwise, there is not much detailed content to these slogans yet.

In foreign policy, where some of the students have been criticized as anti-American or non-anti-totalitarian, their hope of a non-machine society seems to have some special impacts. For example, "peace" seems important to them not for the sake of survival alone, or even chiefly, but because the war machine *is* a machine, perfectly calculated to treat three billion humans like things. And indeed "peace" or "disarmament" per se has recently come to mean much less to the students unless it is closely tied to a decent world for the hungry nations. And "decency" is closely attached to the hope that the Third World can create "human" societies that avoid the "machine" mistakes of the West, Russia, and possibly—they plead ignorance—China.

Indeed, those who attack the students for not opposing totalitarianism in the Third World should understand that many of the students have in mind something quite special when they think or speak of "totalitarianism." They mean the generally machine-like, dehumanizing quality of great bureaucracies, not the specially dehumanizing system of secret police and thought control. This is one of the most important aspects of their thought, and is why some of them can in one breath damn the University of California as "totalitarian" and deny that Cuba is. For Cuba seems to be "turned on," live, unbureaucratic, full of sex and unexpectedness, even if its government controls the press; but the multiversity is gray and chilly.

Given a choice between psychological repression and political suppression, the students would choose to be suppressed. And this is not simply a leftward favoritism: the students fight the racist and anti-civil-libertarian government of Mississippi, but they save their deepest fury for the cool, gray way in which the Justice Department in Washington refuses to come to their aid. And they find a joy in working in Mississippi, beatings, jail and all, that they would never find as cool gray bureaucrats in Washington.

The students respond to a wide range of issues in explicitly "moral" terms rather than strategic or technical ones. "Is it right?" not "Will it work?" "They are disgusting" not "They are stupid." I think there is a strong component of Gandhi, or Gandhianized Christianity, or Gandhi-Camus existentialism in this. Not that they are pure Gandhians by any means. But they tend to believe that it is not always, or even usually, possible to work out the impact given means will have on hoped-for ends, and thus to choose means on some intrinsic moral principle— if not absolute nonviolence, then a "not-quite-violent" ethic. They have not much understanding of the real meaning of Dewey's pragmatism as regards the relation between ends and means, as far as I can tell; and they seem to be dubious of spelling out their ultimate ends, partly because of an existentialist focus on *Now* and partly because spelling out goals might result in the mistaken exclusion of some people whose ends would grow and change if they shared in action instead of being excluded.

They are self-activating. Unlike SANE and CORE at one level of the political spectrum, ADA at another, or the 1948 Progressive Party at still another, they seem *not* to have been put into motion by an older generation of people who had very clearly worked-out ideologies and who, at least for a long time, kept basic control of the organizations they created.

The student movements are different from all of them in that the group that created them is at most ten years older than the *youngest* of the members, and the founder group is still working out its own ideology. In SDS there is now a cadre with opinions and analyses much more "sophisticated" than those of the new entrants—but the cadre itself is under 30 and is still creating its own ideology.

It is this whole atmosphere of self-creation that makes for the

87

self-confident feeling among the students that no one else could "infiltrate" or control them. It is far more likely that the student movements will end up creating and giving the basic tone to and thus perhaps for a long time "controlling" other organizations, as for example the Mississippi Freedom Party, the Newark Community Union (in the slums), even conceivably faculty groups that take both their *élan* and their office workers from their students—than that anyone will be able to control them.

Their ideology and rhetoric urges them to work towards decentralizing their own organizations and to avoid imposing their own ideas on the groups they are organizing—especially the ideologically defenseless ones in the slums and the Delta. But in fact, of course, there are enormous internal pressures to assume that they are right and to make the new groups in the images that seem appropriate to the founders, as the founders tried to make SANE and CORE and Turn Toward Peace. Nevertheless, it always *tends* to be "legitimate" among the students to uphold decentralization and oppose a central bureaucracy, and always "illegitimate" to want to read somebody out for disagreement on what needs doing or how to do it. (Not that it never happens.) This results, on the one hand, in its being difficult to "control" the student organizations themselves. On the other, it results in things happening that look to some outsiders like "infiltration," and that no one in the organization will repudiate because of respect and tenderness for the "commitment" and world-view of others.

One of the strongest of their commitments—both in general ideology and in their own organizational work—is the ethic of personal warmth. That is, deep respect (not just tolerance) for personal peculiarities, an atmosphere of love and gentleness towards each other, and an unwillingness to interfere with love affairs, dress, or personal oddities even if these seemed to be getting in the way of the movement as a political thrust. Efforts to advance the personal happiness of the members of the movement have seemed as important as formal victories in the society. Asceticism was a matter of individual choice or of scarce resources, not of puritanical discipline. The ethic of personal warmth may be declining—I think I detect this, but I'm not sure —as work in the ghettoes gets tougher and the demand for superhuman energy and commitment grows. But some of the students have already seen this "danger" and are trying to counteract it by bringing artists, actors, and other specially non-puritanical or non-political people into the ghetto projects. Again, what they fear worst is grayness and sameness.

If the commitment to personal warmth survives for the next five years, it is likely to have major political implications. For one thing, most Americans—even those who fully enjoy the blessings of *liberté* and *égalité*—seem to feel a lack of *fraternité* in their lives. If the movement can offer this to them, so that as Carmine de Sapio offered jobs as patronage and Franklin Roosevelt offered the welfare state as patronage, the movement would be offering *love* as its patronage, then many older Americans may join it.

Already the students have been able to attract, and to accept as equals in the movement, people who are no longer or never were in college. The movement began by offering older adolescents a new sort of identity to choose at just that moment in their own life histories when, according to Eriksonian theory, they would have been searching for an identity. It has grown by offering older Negroes a chance to cast off their stifling old identities—and people like Fannie Lou Hamer have responded. It has grown by offering older academics a chance to rework their professional identities (developed in a blinkered race through college and graduate school as mere early rungs on the occupational ladder) by joining science to social action as if they were still students—and people like those who invented the teach-ins have responded. It has begun to offer a similar redefinition of identity and self to older clergymen—and many of them responded at Selma.

To the degree that the movement can keep its sense of community, its openness to experiment, its refusal to dogmatize, its sense of locality, peculiarity, and its willingness to accept recruits who come from right or left without demanding a prior conversion—to that extent, it may be able during the next five years to reach up the age range and outside the social range within which it now operates.

Alternatively, the movement could so deeply challenge the established ways of life in America that the powers of the press, the purse, and ultimately the police are turned against it. Such an outcome is somewhat more likely—not inevitable—if, for example, the war in Vietnam continues and intensifies; for the students are deeply committed to oppose it, and few societies in time of war can stomach a challenge to the war itself or to their established ways of doing business. If they were to be confronted with a society that was moving not to join with them but to suppress them, the students might then find their own behavior changing in ways that would now horrify them. Their openness might turn to secrecy, their experimental mood to doctrinaire hostility, their hoμe to bitterness, their dissent to treason, and then indeed the process of suppression would speed up.

The responsibility for preventing such a disaster rests in part on the students themselves, since such a change would betray their own system of values. But that responsibility rests also in part on the rest of American society, which would have broken and thrown aside the most vigorous expression of its own next generation.

11

Notes on a Trial Near Wall Street

Perhaps the least publicized political trial recently held in the United States ended on December 20, [1965], in the Criminal Court of New York City, ordinarily a most publicity-minded metropolis. It ended with the acquittal of the defendants—seventeen young men and women who "sat out" last March 19 on the sidewalk next to the headquarters building of the Chase Manhattan Bank, a tall and glassy structure in the heart of the financial district. Under the sponsorship of Students for a Democratic Society, they were memorializing the Sharpeville massacre of 1960, in which South African police killed 72 black Africans. They were doing so at the Chase Manhattan Bank instead of the South African consulate because they wanted the Chase to stop lending money to the South African government.

The seventeen defendants were left from several hundred pickets, forty-nine sit-outers, and a delegation of five students who had met with the vice-chairman of the Chase's board. All those who sat out on the sidewalk were arrested, charged first with disorderly conduct and then with resisting arrest when they "went limp" instead of walking to the paddy wagons. Most of them pleaded guilty to "disorderly," were give five-day suspended jail sentences, and had the charges of resisting arrest dismissed. But the stubborn seventeen argued that since their sit-out did not interrupt traffic on the sidewalk or to and from the bank, they were not being "disorderly" but simply carrying on a more vigorous and uncomfortable form of picketing. They also argued that when they failed to take an active part in making their own arrests, they were not legally "resisting" the police.

The trial of the seventeen was conducted along dry legal lines: Was or was not the traffic blocked? Did or did not a lady *Life* photographer walk freely through the sit-out lines? Were or were not the defendants' arms kept interlocked until after each arrest, so that policemen had to separate them forcibly in order to carry them off? Was or was not the law of New York clear on the meaning of "disorderly conduct" and "resisting arrest"? The court heard hours and days of conflicting testimony on these points, and none at all on the reasons for the demonstration. To the young opponents of apartheid, therefore, the atmosphere of the trial itself became one of overwhelming suffocation. They found that no one else seemed to know or care why they were on trial, and they occasionally began to wonder about it themselves. The trial was not improved by being postponed or interrupted half a dozen times while the prosecutor recovered from the flu, while a defense attorney arbitrated a labor case, while the judge (John Murtagh) gave a lecture in Boston, while one young defendant took Regents' examinations, while an older one ran CORE's national convention. Indeed, the trial became so suffocating that one defendant remarked morosely, "I thought Kafka was writing *The Trial* about life in general. I guess he meant the administration of justice after all."

The defendants were kept going only by the hope that they could establish the legitimacy and legality of sidewalk sit-downs and going limp, at least under New York law and possibly under the Federal Constitution. They, and their lawyers from the American Jewish Committee and the Workers' Defense League, hoped to make it possible for many other sorts of demonstrations, especially over civil rights and racial equality, to use some of the new techniques of vigorous public protest without being harassed by charges of disorderly conduct and resisting arrest. Few of the defendants hoped to get their point accepted by the trial judge; and they were astonished when he dryly said, "The motion before the Court is to dismiss the charges on the ground that the prosecution has failed to prove its case beyond a reasonable doubt. The Court being in reasonable doubt, the motion is granted." So the stubborn seventeen won their point. But, dedicated though they were to this rather abstract and distant goal of broadening the boundaries of legal protest, many of them still felt wistfully that whereas the demonstration itself was liberating, its freedom had been suffocated in the atmosphere of law.

The moments that the sit-down defendants remember are the moments in which fear, joy, and passion all mingled last spring. The first was that moment early in the day when the students were given first-grade training in nonviolence by a high-school boy, who had been through previous demonstrations with Friends of S.N.C.C. He quietly and matter-of-factly explained that the New York police might beat them, and showed them how males on the sit-down line could stay next to girls so as to be able to interpose their own nonviolent bodies if the girls should become special targets for billy clubs. Then, as the tension grew and his fellow "adolescents" visibly tried to take their courage in their hands, he ended the demonstration lesson by laughing, "Now remember—stay nonviolent and *maintain your cool.*" Then there was the moment when the police arrived and the students, in the midst of "We Shall Overcome," switched to the verse that says "We are not afraid"—and sang it three times, quavering on every note. And the moment when, having been hauled away (with kid gloves to their astonishment) they asked a jailer why the cells were so clean and were told, "But *nobody* gets arrested on Wall Street." And the moment, finally, when the men were brought from their separate cells to be arraigned—and responded to the first faraway sounds of female singing with a joyful rush to the bars of their own large cage and a joyful outpouring of love, relief, and warmth, in some triumphant singing of their own.

That last occasion provides a key to much in the student movement. As one defendant said in awe, "Now I know what Freud meant by *Eros:* not just sex, but tenderness and renewal and communitas and 'overcoming,' and sex too." For what is perhaps most distinctive about the politics of the student movement is that it offers a sense of community and love—Freud's *Eros*—to its members and to those who might join in.

Even if what holds the movement together is the exhilaration of risking life and limb (or trying to) and doing this together, "in community," presumably that was not the chief purpose of the Chase Manhattan demonstration. Not that the student lead-

93

ers expected the Chase to see the light and end its loans to South Africa. But they did expect to raise questions in the minds of the Chase, of the financial and political communities in general, and of students and other citizens who had never before confronted the issue of American responsibility in dealing with apartheid; and this they accomplished. At the most immediate level, the New York *Times* reported that securities dealers were "more interested in the picketing in front of the Chase Manhattan Bank building than in the bond market."

In the broader sense, the written and photographic coverage of the event by the New York papers may have signalled to some readers that a new issue had entered the universe of "demonstration" causes that had previously included only civil rights, peace, and the free university. To this extent, the demonstration may have called to public attention not only the system of apartheid in South Africa but the system of rationalization and denial by which American support for apartheid is permitted to continue.

But perhaps more important than even this public notice was the effect of the demonstration on the campuses. A number of students who took part reported that on their campuses, some faculty and students responded to information about American business support of apartheid with an even deeper sense of moral outrage than they ordinarily gave either to racial inequality within the United States or to the war in Vietnam. Evidently, there were some academics who felt that horrors born of "tragic necessity" in Southeast Asia or of "an improving mess" in Mississippi paled before the deliberate, systematic, and worsening horrors of apartheid. This resonance that the Chase Manhattan, South Africa issue had on campus may well presage an American anti-apartheid campaign; and that is important enough. But perhaps even more important, it indicated that some of the same students who were being criticized as "neo-isolationists" for opposing the war in Vietnam were actually deeply concerned with the correct and worthwhile use of American power to make the world more decent—a kind of "neo-interventionism."

Not that most of the students willingly or easily see themselves as the new bearers of the American mission. Some would agree that what they are doing is helping to bring about a democratic (and if possible a nonviolent) revolution in South Africa before there is a totalitarian one, perhaps Communist-oriented; and that they are using and urging the use of the means that have been made at least semi-legitimate by the civil-rights movement —sit-ins, economic boycotts, and so on—to achieve ends, such as liberty and racial equality, that are fully legitimate American ideals. These, who would recognize themselves as "neo-interventionists," distinguish the government's military intervention in Vietnam from what they want in South Africa, on the grounds that only an intervention using nonmilitary, libertarian means can hope to produce a democratic result.

Many other students, on the other hand, might accept the "neo-isolationist" label. They see the Chase Manhattan demonstration as a demand only that Americans stop supporting evil elsewhere, not that they get involved in bringing about the good society elsewhere. Many of them believe that America is so wealthy, conservative, and stuffy that it cannot help but misunderstand and damage the hungry nations, even when it intends to help them. And America should, therefore, simply, disengage itself from the "Third World." They would reject the rhetoric of the "American mission"—a rhetoric which makes them especially uncomfortable because they identify it with their opponents inside the Chase Manhattan.

But it is possible to make an independent assessment of the political results of what even the neo-isolationists actually do, rather than what they say. Such an assessment strongly suggests that all of the students—neo-isolationists as well as neo-interventionists—are in fact acting out of their roles as Americans, out of American ideals that date back to Jefferson and Thoreau and William Lloyd Garrison. It is these American ideals that they are trying to get South Africa to begin to approach, and in this sense all of them are indeed bearers of the American mission. Thus the Chase Manhattan demonstration exposed an ambivalence about the values of the American tradition (which are respected) and of the American present (which are scorned) that simultaneously puts the student movement under considerable strain and energizes it to new action.

In the case of the South Africa demonstrations, more was at work in the heads of the project's originators than the ending of racism in South Africa, or the ending of American support for it, or even the focusing of attention on American relations with the Third World in general. They wanted to focus attention on the Chase not only because it was the largest contributor to an American bank consortium that bailed out the South African economy after the Sharpeville massacre had badly damaged confidence in the South African future, but because the Chase—a Rockefeller bank—had a reputation not for right-wing fanaticisms but for forward-looking policies: in the students' outlook, it was an example of "liberal corporatism."

Some of the student organizers wanted, in short, to make it publicly clear that one need not be a rabid racist to support the horrors of apartheid—and indeed that the support crucial to continuing apartheid might well come from respectable, "forward-looking" American institutions. This emphasis was the measure of their distrust of and disgust for the official institutions of the American present; and they felt that their suspicions had been confirmed when the Chase went to court seeking an injunction against the public criticism of its loans to South Africa —even against the wearing of buttons with the inscription, "Chase Manhattan—Partner in Apartheid." (The bank's request was refused, but the students were enjoined against demonstrating inside the bank itself, as they had planned to do. That is why they ended up in a "sit-out" on the pavement just outside.)

It is this disgust for the present forms of American society that has fueled one constant tension within the movement: the debate —often subvocal, often within single individuals, rather than among them—between defining the American rhetoric of the free society as a phony veneer for the disgusting reality, or regarding the rhetoric of the free society as the deeper reality, to be used in transforming institutions so as to make them more nearly like their ideal selves.

In beginning their efforts to bring the rhetorical American opposition to apartheid into political reality, students from S.D.S. first did a remarkable amount of research into the connections between American business and industry and the South African financial system. They also drew on the findings of the British anti-apartheid movement, especially the Penguin collection on *Sanctions Against South Africa,* edited by Ronald Segal. They found two documents most useful in organizing on the campuses. One was a tough-minded description of the interlocking directorates involved in a great part of the American investment in South Africa, with the Chase Manhattan Bank and Charles W. Engelhard, chairman of Dillon, Read & Co. and a prominent New Jersey Democrat, sharing the center of the stage. The other was a collection of affidavits by African prisoners who had been arrested or imprisoned for membership in various anti-apartheid or nationalist organizations, describing in detail the tortures to which they had been subjected—either to extort confessions of sabotage and treason or simply as punishment. In this second paper there were no comments, no embellishment; there did not need to be. When the two papers were circulated together, they generated considerable shock and indignation. Since the first report named a good many companies other than the Chase Manhattan that were intimately involved in the South African trade, students outside New York were able to pick their own local outfit as the focus of protest—and hundreds of them did, in Washington, San Francisco, and many other cities.

Armed thus with the concern of growing numbers of students around the country, S.D.S. entered into discussions with the officers of the Chase Manhattan. They were repeatedly told that the bank did not take sides in political disputes and did not take political issues into account as a reason either to advance or withhold investment funds. (But the bank, in explaining and defending its stand, specified that it had "normal banking relationships with both private and governmental customers in virtually every country outside of the Communist bloc"—thereby hinting that Communism was a political issue that it did take into account.)

The students utterly rejected the no-politics standards, both on the ground that economic decisions *ought* to be based on a vision of good politics and on the ground that in fact financial judgments could not help but have major elements of political judgment and values, as when the Chase decided to bolster the shaky apartheid economy after Sharpeville—when it could have decided instead that in the long run the better financial return would come from encouraging the beginnings of a march away

97

from apartheid and towards the construction of a democratic society in South Africa. On these grounds, then, the students went forward into the demonstration against the Chase and similar supporters of the South African economy.

Since the March demonstrations, the continuing escalation of the war in Vietnam has attracted more and more energy and urgency from S.D.S. and other student activists, with the result that the demand for an immediate anti-apartheid campaign has been muted. But many of the students who were activated by the March demonstrations have not forgotten or abandoned the South African issue. Some of them have discovered that their own colleges are major investors or depositors in the Chase Manhattan Bank (Swarthmore is a prime example), and have begun to demand that such deposits be withdrawn until the Chase stops investing in the apartheid regime. Others have kept on with research into the financial and economic ties of American interests with South Africa, in order to discover which of these interests might be more amenable to persuasion or pressure. There has been some discussion of several possible action projects: for example, citizens of Harlem and other ghettoes in the North might be interested in one or another kind of direct action against American firms doing business with South Africa; that Africanist faculty members might join with interested students to hold teach-ins on South Africa next Sharpeville Week; that scientists in the Space Agency and the Atomic Energy Commission might be interested in protesting racial discrimination in those agencies' installations in South Africa. Some students have begun to think about organizing such protests. None of this ferment has yet ripened into effective action; but the Freedom Movement, as the students call it, is clearly moving towards the demand that Johannesburg be put on the same agenda as Jackson.

12
Notes on New Politics

The Chicago Convention on New Politics, in September 1967,* was built on the assumption that there was one movement, with many parts. Perhaps if we had exposed this assumption to ourselves early in the game, we would have realized that it was a mistake. But we operated on it only half-consciously. I suppose we desperately wanted to believe it: to believe that electoral reformers and radical organizers and Black militants could all become one movement. Certainly the times seemed to require it: the Vietnam War seemed on the verge of a new and finally disastrous escalation—perhaps an invasion to the North; the Black communities had burned down Newark and Detroit. Surely we needed a single movement. $/35864$

The wish was father to the conviction. As a result, we proposed a voting plan whereby every group doing the kind of community-organizing work we defined as "new politics" would have as many votes as it had active, working members. (This was a much wider category than the specifically electoral groups such as the California Community for New Politics, the American Independent Movement in Connecticut, or PAX in Massachusetts.) We assumed that a majority of all the votes cast would reflect the political realities of the American left.

But—as we discovered or were reminded in Chicago—there was not one movement, but two: one Black and one white. Indeed, we should have known—precisely in the wake of Newark and Detroit—that 1967 was the hardest year in American history for Blacks and whites to work together. If we had taken this into account from the first (and I include in this

* In reading this assessment of the Convention, readers should keep in mind that my position there was as a member of the original Convention Steering Committee, a supporter of the "local organizing" perspective, and a white man. There was much, therefore, that other people saw and I did not.

99

"we" the seven Black members of the Convention Steering Committee), we could have proposed some kind of bicameral system at Chicago—a requirement that any decision receive both a Black majority and a white majority, to be considered an act of the whole Convention. But we did not do this, and as a result when the Convention met the mostly white organizations held 28,000 votes, the Black ones that asked for regular credentials about 5,000, and the Black organizations that did not seek regular accreditation probably another 10,000. In short a majority of the whites at the Convention could in theory have bound a majority of the Blacks to a given course of action against their will.

That was politically unrealistic. Among the whites and among the Blacks, minorities might well have accepted the judgment of majorities as to whether the New Politics should or should not mount a Presidential campaign, should or should not pass a given resolution. But the Blacks were not prepared to bow to any majority but their own. In hindsight I must agree—they were right.

As the Convention began, the Blacks who arrived created a Black Caucus. We had assumed, and indeed intended to encourage, the creation of many such caucuses—around special concerns or policies like support for a third Presidential ticket, organizational ties like membership in Women's Strike or the Mobilization, geography. But the Black Caucus from the first acted differently from the other caucuses: it demanded (and was given) a special meeting room, it began to create its own organizational structure, and its members spent their time there rather than in the commissions and plenaries of the regular Convention. Perhaps most important, its members talked little to outsiders about what was going on inside the Caucus—its internal disagreements and political life—and they cast their whole public weight behind the positions adopted by the Caucus majority.

Putting together what little did leak out of the Black Caucus during the Convention, however, and what its members said later about its deliberations, I would tentatively sketch the following picture: there was a policy deadlock inside the Caucus, which found itself divided between Blacks who wanted to participate in the Convention and those who did not. Among the "Separators," some in fact left, and created a Black Convention on the South Side of Chicago. But others stayed, attempting to persuade those Blacks who supported participation that they too should leave. In short, they wanted to leave the Convention, but only if they could take the "participators" with them; Black solidarity came first.

The participators held a precise mirror-image view: they wanted to enter the Convention, but only if they could take the "separators" in with them. Allowing for a number of exceptions, very roughly the separators tended to be Northern-ghetto Black-Power militants, and they argued both that the Convention was stacked against Blacks and that in any case the Black movement should have its own political organization—which had failed to come out of the Newark Black Power Conference. The participators, again very roughly, tended to be Northern poverty workers and most of the Southerners—of which the major organizations were Southern Christian Leadership Conference groups, the Mississippi Freedom Democratic Party, the Lowndes County (Alabama) Freedom Organization, and the Southwest Georgia Project.

The two camps inside the Caucus argued out their position for two days. The "participators" would not participate unless in effect they got permission from the separators; the separators would not leave unless the participators came along. Caught in this strange embrace, they ultimately worked out a solution which discharged their energy upon the white Convention. In effect, the participators proposed to set the white Convention a stiff test: a test defined, indeed, by the toughest criteria the separators could devise. If the Convention passed the test, all of the Black Caucus would enter; if the Convention refused, all of the Caucus would leave. The separators made clear once more that they were not really interested in putting radical tests to the Convention, since they believed a separate Black organization was preferable in any case; but they acceded, and helped work out the test.

The test was the 13-point resolution that the Black Caucus, at 8 P.M. Friday, sent to the Convention staff with the demand that it be passed by 1 P.M. the next day. And at that point the second deep division that possessed the Convention—the one *inside* the white Convention, as the first had been inside the Black Caucus—came into play. That division was between those whites who wanted a third Presidential ticket and those who wanted to spend 1968 in building local organizations, strengthening the movement at its grass roots, rather than in a national Presidential campaign. The spearhead of the local-organizing perspective was the Radical Caucus, made up of Vietnam Summer staff, organizers from the elder-SDS projects in Newark and Chicago, and the younger SDS members who were present at the Convention. The support for a third ticket came from liberal peaceniks such as SANE and Women's Strike; the New Politics groups from California and to some extent Connecticut and Massachusetts; and the small but well-knit complex of the Communist Party and the DuBois Clubs.

Within the white convention, the 13 Points produced remarkably different effects. Only a few points were controversial in themselves, but these were very controversial indeed. Most problematical were condemation of the "imperialistic Zionist war," support for all wars of national liberation, and support of all the resolutions of the Newark Black Power Conference (which none of the whites and few of the Blacks had seen). The condemnation of Israel was by far the toughest sticking point. It had been inserted by the Black Caucus not for any worked-out ideological reason but to establish solidarity with SNCC, which had already taken the same stance, and prevent the political isolation of SNCC in a period of great danger of violence to or police repression of its members. But of course the Israeli point posed deep problems to the white convention. To liberal peaceniks and to the new-politics groups, the point itself was anathema. To the Communists, it was party dogma. To many (but by no means all) of the young radicals, it seemed correct enough to warrant no serious opposition in itself. *But few of these groups voted on the basis of their intrinsic belief in or disagreement with the 13 Points.*

Instead, they voted on the basis of their deep-felt reaction to American racism. Most liberals turned their guilt over racism into an act of penance: they voted for the 13 Points, although they disagreed with them most strongly, because they could not bear to be rejected by the Blacks who would leave the Convention if the 13 Points were voted down. (Many of them, strongly committed to creating a third Presidential ticket, felt that such a ticket needed Black support; and they were willing to go to any length to keep the Blacks inside the Convention.) In effect, the liberals voted to castrate themselves as organizers in the white community because they accepted the responsibility and guilt of American racism.

Radicals, on the other hand—not all of them, perhaps not even a majority, but a much higher proportion than among the liberals—voted against the 13 Points precisely because they felt the Points would make organizing in the white community extremely hard, and because they felt no guilt for American racism. They had turned their guilt not into penance but into action to destroy American racism, did not need for their internal peace the legitimacy of Black partnership in one organization, did not want a third ticket which would require Black support, and indeed tended to believe there should be separate Black and white organizations. Many of them sensed that approval of the 13 Points would be a patronizing gesture towards the Blacks, carrying with it no intention to organize on the basis of such a platform. (Indeed, some people left the Black Caucus after the Convention voted for the 13 Points, muttering as they headed for the Black Convention on the South Side that their passage was a white put-on.)

But despite the opposition of the radicals (and of many of the new-politics people, who were also doing real organizing among whites and therefore felt little need to discharge guilt in penitential self-castration), the liberals carried the day—and the 13 Points.* A *de facto* alliance of Black moderates and white liberals had combined to impose an "ultra" piece of rhetoric on themselves—against the wishes of most Black and white radicals.

---

* I still think that one decent and workable policy would have been the one I proposed to a number of people and groups at the Convention but could not—irony of ironies in a convention many felt was "controlled" by the Steering Committee—get the floor to propose to the whole Convention. That was to adopt the 13 Points as a legitimate statement of one wing of the movement and to adopt simultaneously a radical statement for the "white" wing, covering many of the same issues but couched in language intended to arouse energies for organizing in white communities.

The process of struggle and conflict had its own effects upon the liberals. Many of them learned a great deal from the raw fact of challenge from the powerless—learned, for example, that a united tough minority committed not to obeying the rules but to changing them can sometimes win its way. (A lesson some began to apply to themselves, in the larger context of America.) Other began to realize what they had done to themselves as organizers by adopting the 13 Points, and moved past the guilt-penance point to a concern with effective action. As they did, their thoughts merged into the Convention's second great debate: between the local-organizing and the third-ticket perspectives. And the context in which that debate happened allowed the debate further to radicalize some of the liberals.

The third ticket was supported by peacenik liberals who wanted to defeat Johnson, and new-politics groups like the Berkeley Community for New Politics that were well-enough organized at their own base to believe a presidential campaign both made sense and might help them. It was opposed by radicals who focused not on beating Johnson but on changing America, and whose constituencies were so far behind Berkeley that they saw a presidential campaign as a drain on resources badly needed for local organizing, not as an addition to them. The long discussions of this issue on the floor and in the corridors, especially in the aftermath of the fight over the 13 Points, helped many liberals to see the country's need as deeper than the defeat of Johnson. If the local-organizing people had made clear their great interest in local electoral politics, they would probably have won by a considerable majority. As it was, starting from behind they achieved a bare majority of 2 votes out of 27,000 cast. The new-politics groups then shifted position enough to arrange a compromise. It encouraged Presidential tickets in only those states where the new politics was strongest. The compromise was so shaky that it really satisfied neither the localist nor third-ticket people; but it stood till the next day.

It was on the next day that "the Black Caucus question" revived. The Caucus demanded to receive credentials as a bloc incorporating all the Black organizations originally present, and to receive as many votes as all the white delegations put together.

Whether to appove this made up the third crucial fight of the Convention. It had much the quality of the first, except that many people felt the 50% demand was more nearly legitimate (as an expression of the equal strength of the two movements) than the 13 Points had been. Yet fewer people voted for it— an index to the change of gut feeling from the day before, as some liberals became more nearly working radicals.

As the Caucus won its 28,000 votes, many delegates feared it would either throw its weight to one of the two different perspectives that had divided the whites (thereby dictating a course of action that most of the whites opposed) or would destroy the Convention in contempt for the way in which the whites had damaged themselves. But the Blacks did neither. Instead, the controlling force in the Caucus—now for the first time seen clearly by outsiders to be the "moderates"—acted to strengthen the compromise perspective and to try to create a viable structure for NCNP. The last day of the Convention thus felt like a time of reconciliation and final re-education.

But the movement was never the same. The fleeting possibility of a new coalition between the politicians of creative disorder and those of electoral reform disappeared. White liberals who remained liberals found themselves burned so badly by attempts to work with Blacks that they fled any such alliance. White radicals felt challenged to build much stronger bases in the white community before seeking alliances with the marching Blacks. And the Blacks learned how to create Black Caucuses in dozens of organizations that could demand change great enough to be useful but not so great as to destroy the organization. Almost everyone in the movement learned a great deal. But NCNP of course collapsed.

13
Gandhi and Guerrilla

The Pentagon siege [of November 21–22, 1967] can be treated as a tactical event to be analyzed and criticized as one possible model for future physical confrontations. This is a necessary process: there will be more occasions for physical confrontations and they ought to be much better planned than the Pentagon was. Can we do better at the Democratic National Convention in Chicago? What if we use snake dances? And so on. Points to remember:

1. Tactically rather than politically speaking, the Pentagon was a bad choice for resistance—if by that we mean events like the siege, not simply symbolic arrests. The Pentagon is a fort, the Potomac its moat. Urban settings should be more vulnerable.

2. Simple logistical preparation—blankets, canteens and so forth—would have helped.

3. So would knowledge of stress psychology—such as the despondency characteristic of the last hour before dawn, and how to combat it.

4. Although physical confrontations may have to be commanded at the last moment by a previously selected "college of generals," this ought not to push the Movement toward letting a small élite take over decision-making before or after the confrontation itself. If not guarded against, this could happen fairly easily—especially if physical confrontations play a larger and larger role in the life of the movement.

But the siege can also be seen as a microcosm of the *political* situation: and this seems much more important to me.

The siege was a crude, unplanned mixture of Gandhi and guerrilla. That mixture is what made it a success. Neither the Gandhiism (*à la* Dave Dellinger's teach-in and early arrest) nor the guerrilla-style hostility (*à la* the efforts of the Revolutionary Contingent to charge the troops) worked or could have worked

106

either morally or politically—if used alone by one or another group of the demonstrators. We now ought to examine the rough guerrilla-Gandhi mixture and try to develop a true synthesis of the two approaches. (I don't know myself, yet, what that means; but I feel a need for not throwing away either side of what we did on the Mall.)

What I mean by the mixture: people half walked through, half charged through the outer troop lines and frequently went around them—through the bushes. They did not wait to convert or convince or use soul-force upon those troops. Yet once they reached the Mall they established their empathy with the troops, made clear they saw The Enemy as generals and presidents rather than soldiers, and set a crowd discipline that prevented the use of violence even when U.S. marshals beat demonstrators in full sight of the crowd. (One group of sit-downers even re-fused to move to a tactically more useful spot because they said they had established a warm emotional connection with "their" soldiers, and would not leave them.) And since it became pos-sible to express and use the Gandhian commitment effectively only once people had got up to the Mall, I am saying that on Saturday evening the guerrilla approach was the correct fulfill-ment of Gandhian intentions.

On the other hand, I think it was a mistake on Sunday morn-ing to follow guerrilla modes of thought with the same rigidity as the majority did when it decided to leave the Mall at 6 o'clock. The decision was urged and justified by some of the S.D.S. leadership as returning the initiative to the Movement rather than the Pentagon and exemplifying the guerrilla tactic of strike-retreat-and-strike-again. But the results were that six hundred to a thousand people, who probably could have been kept to-gether till the sunrise restored their morale, were instead en-couraged to retreat (though in fairly good order) and that the S.D.S. national leadership did not go to jail, which in *this* particu-lar case—given that jail meant two to five days rather than two to five years—was a political as well as moral error. Staying out of jail separated the leaders from some of the Movement during days when they could have carried on important political educa-tion and re-established moral solidarity. Furthermore, the coun-try was not forced to address the meaning of a really massive

107

two-day occupation of the Mall, followed by large-scale arrests and perhaps a jail-no-bail movement. In short, I am saying that on Sunday morning the Gandhian approach would have been the wisest guerrilla tactic to use, for those who thought in political guerrilla terms, as well as the morally correct one for those who thought in essentially religious terms.

More generally, I would argue that in the present state of the Movement and the country, precisely because large parts of our movement are moving to resistance, with its guerrilla overtones, it is important for us not to forget the central meaning of the Gandhian approach: that those we must oppose are not The Enemy. Certainly this is true as regards the "great center" of American society, whether or not it is true of the "power elite." If it is these large numbers of the unconvinced whom we must transform if we are to end the war and make any more such wars impossible, then we cannot treat them as our enemies. We must get through to them what we mean; we must be able to remake their ideas of what legitimate behavior is so that what we do—not what the police and the President do—is felt to be legitimate.

I emphasize this because I have talked with some people who took part in the Pentagon siege who bitterly reacted to the press distortions of the siege. They felt that if efforts to build community with the soldiers could be described as "taunts" and if the demonstrators' fantastic restraint in the face of police violence could be described as initiating violence, then there was no point to trying so hard—that "America" would define what we do as illegitimate regardless of what it is we do. I do not agree with this. I think that if we stay inside truly legitimate bounds (based on our own moral sense), we will be able to bring the press and the country to join us. Not in one go-round, of course; naturally the press would define as "violence" the most direct challenge Americans have made to the legitimacy of their own government since South Carolina fired on Fort Sumter, even though we were *not* firing on the Pentagon. But just as those who once condemned mass marches for withdrawal as "irresponsible" now applaud them as "moderate," so those who now are horrified by resistance will come to understand it.

The real problem is, what do *we* feel is legitimate? And here we falter. There are a few of us who feel that July 6, 1775, has already arrived and a "Declaration of the Causes and Necessity of Taking Up Arms" well justified. A few of us feel that July 6 can never arrive in that sense, because the taking up of arms is never wholly justified (though perhaps defensible). And more of us are not certain what to think: but we are *acting* as if violence were not legitimate.

(If one rereads the declarations both of 1775 and 1776 with these moral and political dilemmas on one's mind, they come alive in some new ways. People who have struggled with whether to "support the National Liberation Front" and what that means, can understand why the Declaration of Independence specifies that the colonies may make alliances with foreign powers: imagine the emotional strain on Englishmen born and bred of deciding whether to commit treason in the company of the hereditary enemy, France! And it is important to see that even in the moment of rebellion, the colonists did not treat all Britain as The Enemy or dismiss the possibility of making themselves seem legitimate to their opponents. Instead they specified the King as enemy, and carefully wrote the Declaration to explain and justify their acts and to claim legitimacy for themselves.)

What might we put in a Declaration on the Causes and Necessity of Resistance? I would identify three levels of resistance: withdrawal, challenge and coercion, and I would endorse the first two while rejecting the third. Here is why:

On *withdrawal:* simply, it is a crime to fight in the American war against Vietnam; therefore it is no crime to refuse the draft. It is a crime to pay for that war; therefore it cannot be a crime to refuse taxes.

On *challenge:* when we attempt to block the Pentagon with our bodies, or interfere with an induction center or a napalm plant or a campus recruiting booth, we are saying something very special—so long as we do not initiate violence in the process. We are saying, "We will not literally *force* you to stop the Pentagon, but we will force you to use violence on us in order to keep the Pentagon going—just as you use violence on the Vietnamese. We believe that, confronted with such a direct challenge from ever-growing numbers (though a minority) of Americans, the majority will decide to stop: will decide that if killing Vietnamese

109

requires beating and arresting Americans, the killing of Vietnamese should end." It should be noted that even if these challenges are carried on with the greatest toughness and energy—like the Pentagon siege, and more—they are still basically a tactic of persuasion. They are built on the assumption that it is legitimate to be arrested if one violates what seems to be the law, though of course the validity of the law should then be challenged in court.

Finally, what about *coercion?* Here I would draw the line—not necessarily forever, but for now. Given a clear and deliberate decision by the majority of the American people to commit major crimes against another people (or part of its own people), it might become legitimate for a minority to try to prevent such crimes from taking place. But that is not our case. On the last occasion the American people had a chance to decide on war or peace—in 1964—they decided for peace. If they get a chance to make that decision again, in 1968, and decide to support war criminals; or if they decide to end war crimes but their decision is ignored as their last one was; or if they are denied, and cannot create, a way to make a decision on those issues—then this last issue will have to be rethought. (Why give the system another chance? Because any body politic is liable to be tricked and defrauded once; if it allows this to happen twice, it has abandoned the effort to restore democracy. If it deliberately chooses war crimes, then its democratic-ness is irrelevant.)

But there is every evidence that the American people, confronted with the overwhelming facts that their government is perpetrating war crimes and that a rising proportion of their compatriots are prepared to resist those crimes, are now trying to reinvent the democratic process. They are patriots, and it helps to know that the resisters are patriots too. And if our commitment to our country sometimes becomes unclear to them, it is *our* job to illuminate it—as we did instinctively on the Pentagon Mall when we sang "America the Beautiful."

This determined effort to restore representative democracy and get it to end the war is being honorably expressed (though some of us may think its premises short-sighted and its means ineffectual) in the various "dump-Johnson" organizations. It seems very likely that the liberals who have in two Mobilizations marched alongside those committed to resistance will now be moving out of the "protest-march" syndrome into political action. (It is not only the resistance people who have concluded that protest is not enough.) Our attitude towards these people will be important—to them and to us. It is almost certainly a mistake to try to keep an organized coalition with them; indeed, the worst errors of the direct-action part of the Mobilization were probably a result of the agonizing negotiations over a period of months between people who wanted direct action and people who didn't. The hauling and shoving prevented a careful and detailed working-out of how to make the direct action fully effective. Now that both wings of the Mobilization are clearly moving forward in different directions (both politics and resistance are "forward" from protest), the old coalition will be even more difficult and even less relevant. But a warm and open-ended communication is much more important than ever.

We may find that we meet each other again in Chicago—not at a New Politics convention this time, but at the Democratic National Convention, because the tactical situation will be good and the Convention is a crucial point in the process by which Johnson might again take power. (The Black movement may join us too.) What should the terms of this meeting be? If there are 100,000 people on the streets, prepared to do civil disobedience, what should their demands be? To most anti-war Americans, the Democratic Party probably does not seem to be intrinsically evil, like the Pentagon; so an unconditional effort simply to block it would seem unreasonable. But what about a demand that the Convention adjourn in favor of an emergency national primary to nominate the Democratic candidates and vote for or against a peace platform? (The demand will seem especially reasonable if Johnson has lost a number of primaries but is about to be nominated by the machine anyway.) What about a demand that delegations from each state have a proportion of Black people equal to the proportion of the Democratic vote cast by Blacks in those states? These notions are only initial speculations; the point is that some way should be sought to keep the hopes and demands of the resistance and the political movements reasonably complementary to each other.

To this point I have assumed that the resistance movement will

111

stay mostly on the campus. But there might be conditions under which the liberal middle class would join it. The chief of these is the possibility of a major escalation of the war—the use of nuclear weapons, a land invasion of the North, or an attack on China. The Consultation on the Church and Society held in Detroit October 23–26, 1967, for example, proposed that the National Council of Churches call a national general strike if any of these three escalations occur (and start preparing now for the possibility). If the middle class does move towards resistance, it will probably be in nonphysical ways: tax refusal, phone-ins to the New York Stock Exchange or the White House, and so on. That likelihood makes even sharper the necessity of viewing the Pentagon siege as a political, not merely a tactical, model from which to learn and advance.

14
Where the Peace Action Is

To understand what has been going on in various forms of action for peace in the country, it may help to sketch what has been going on in the country as a whole—its social make-up over the past generation and pointers towards its social adaptation over the next generation. That is the real base for the emergence of a serious set of peace movements. (Note the plural: there is not really one movement.)

1. THE SOCIAL BASES OF PEACE-SEEKING

When one looks at the social location of Americans over the past generation, one sees three major changes.

First, one can see the emergence of what David Bazelon has called the *new class*. These are people whose property is their education, what they carry around in their heads, not people whose property is shops or farms or stores. Nor are they propertyless people as were the old working class. The new class is not yet self-conscious about its common interests.

Second, we are much more aware of what Gunnar Myrdal in recent years has called the *underclass*. The underclass are really cut off from the mobility system in American society. Increasingly, though not wholly, they are identified by racial as well as by economic deprivation. (That is, a very large proportion of them are Black or Spanish-speaking, and many of the rest are Appalachians.) These people for the first time have become fully conscious of their cut-offness and have begun to develop a sense of cohesion that did not exist in America before. The new class has hardly developed that sense yet.

And third, one sees a change in the holdings of that group of Americans which have for quite a while controlled the workings of the national government. These might be called the *overclass* in America, identifiable as a group of people that have had very considerable power in the shaping of America's domestic and foreign policies since World War II years and probably longer, the group that Galbraith identified as the "New York foreign policy syndicate." (It sounds like rather old-fashioned radical rhetoric, but when a new-fashioned economist and social analyst like Galbraith identifies it, perhaps we should not ignore it.)

One of my colleagues, Richard Barnet, is analyzing the makeup of what he calls the national security managers. He has discovered that there is a group of foreign policy influentials— air commuters to Washington—that constitutes an establishment. They "own" the private and public foreign-policy machinery of the United States because they are the prime movers of the re- sources. They own both the means of production and the means of destruction. That last aspect is the new addition to their hold- ings. It is a peculiarly ambiguous one, because the means of destruction have grown so overwhelming, in what Walter Millis has called the hypertrophy of war, that they have become less and less useful as instruments of policy.

The advent of new kinds of weapons and the increased pro- portion within the American social system of a chunk of the society dedicated to weaponry is absolutely new from 1940 on. Before 1940 the proportion of GNP in the United States devoted to weapons for the Armed Forces never rose above 3 % for more than two or three years at a time (during earlier wars). From 1940 on, there is an entire generation in which the average is 10 % of GNP for the military; and that is a major new de- parture in social structure.

Now, these three big events in American society in the last generation have created their own follow-on events of several kinds. Of special interest are the minority results: that is, what these new events have done to minorities within each of the three classes.

First, some members of the establishment or *overclass* have decided that the ownership of a war system of the kind they own is no longer useful for their own purposes. One begins to see the attempt to invent other ways of carrying on a foreign policy (Peace Corps, space race, and so on). One begins to see the de-

114

tachment of some overclass people from the assumption that the way to manage an international system is to be prepared to go to war under all circumstances. In a sense, those people are a kind of peace movement.

Secondly, the *new class*. The majority of the new class is bureaucratic, nurtured by the multiversity and taught by it to create, as alumni, miniature multiversities in business, government, and education—quite bureaucratic ones. It fills the ranks of big governments, especially big local governments such as huge school systems and social welfare structures.

What is new, again as a *minority* takeoff, are the people of the new class who are breaking loose. Using the facts that their property is in their heads and not tangible, and that they can add to it by doing all sorts of new and interesting things, indeed they leave the bureaucracies and do the new and interesting things. One finds a Tom Hayden deciding in the midst of graduate school that he wants to go into the ghetto of Newark and from there to Hanoi and then back to the ghetto of Newark. Since his property is in his head, he is not even suffering in economic potential or in prestige from doing that. If five years from now for some remarkable reason a Tom Hayden decided that he wanted to be employed by IBM, he would be an even more valuable addition to IBM for having done these things than if he had stayed on in graduate school, because he had added a different kind of property to his head. So one finds not only the older bureaucrats in the new class but these new free men as well—as I emphasized, this is a minority development—and these new free men are again a different kind of peace movement.

For one important thing about the new class is that it is the most transnationally living of classes. Transnational people spend time overseas actually drenched in another society, not simply touring it, but living in it, attempting to understand its value system, deriving a different view of the world from that which assumes that their own national government is always right about foreign policy. Transnational people are able to make the kind of criticisms that have to undergird a peace movement inside a country that has a war potential. Not only is this literally true of persons who live transnationally, but also it is possible to live in one's head transnationally—for some new class people, at

115

least. It was not possible for the older businessmen or the factory workers.

For instance, the beginnings of the teach-in at the University of Michigan were rooted in a group of professors who had access to other than American information about the war in Vietnam, who could read other languages, who had read reports of scholars and journalists who had been to Vietnam, or who themselves had been to Vietnam as economists or social scientists. Such transnational people responded almost as much to the State Department's White Paper (February, 1965) about the war as they did to the war itself, because they were professionally outraged by the White Paper. It was a rationale for U.S. intervention in Vietnam that was intended to snow the informed public, and that was a professional outrage because it was such a weak lie. That is, it was a professional outrage to try to palm off on them a clear set of lies about the origin and nature of the war in Vietnam, when they could go to their sources and show that it was not that. Their new classness was outraged, their very property was affronted, by the attempt to pass off as truth a set of very shaky assumptions about the war. They responded almost as much in outrage about that as in outrage about the actual war itself.

Thirdly, out of the American underclass has begun to come in the '60s a movement which might be said to have a revolutionary trajectory whether or not it has a revolutionary possibility and a revolutionary form. That is true whether it uses non-violence or violence, at least if one believes that Gandhi's attempts at winning independence through nonviolence were a kind of revolution. (The Indian independence movement did not change the Indian social structure very much, but the American Revolution didn't drastically change American social structure either.) But if one accepts nonviolent resistance as a kind of revolution, then certainly what has gone on in Black America (and less so in Spanish-speaking underclass America in California and the Puerto Rican areas of the Northern cities and even more slowly, in that other ethnic group of the underclass, the Appalachian whites, both in the mountain states and in colonies in the big cities such as the North Side of Chicago) promises a quasi-revolutionary trajectory among the underclass. Now, even that development is a minority movement. The majority tendency is still to be in the underclass, still to be cut off, still to be hopeless, still to be apathetic, still to be casually and sporadically and unfocusedly violent, rather than aiming any energy at political change.

The underclass also has characteristics of a peace movement, for two reasons. First, it exerts increasing pressure for redirection of American energies into restructuring American society. The assertive underclass groups vigorously protest the 10 % of GNP that goes into the war system. Their pressure demands that there be serious investment at the floor of American society. Second, the American underclass has an increasing commitment to the world underclass, and therefore an increasing transnationalism of a special sort—commitment to the Third World of economically and racially dispossessed peoples. Among the underclass, one recognizes a growing sense of solidarity with Africa, certainly, and also Latin America and Asia. This at least acts as a peace movement in opposition to some conceivable American wars, namely, United States actions against some African, Latin American, and Asian efforts at social change.

Indeed, the most detailed, most sophisticated study of public opinion on the Vietnam war to date (done by a group centered around Paul Ekman *et al.,* with the participation of the National Opinion Research Center) came up with the fact that the single most predictive variable about opinion concerning the war in Vietnam is race. More predictive even than sex, though sex was second—women tended slightly to be more against the war than men of the same social class, education, and so on. The strongest single predictor, if all other variables are held equal, is that Black people are more likely to be against the war than white people. That was true all up and down the social scale. It is probably much truer now than in the spring of 1966 when the study was made. The San Francisco referendum on immediate withdrawal of American troops from Vietnam, for example, shows a massive majority support for that policy among Black people, much larger than among other social groups.

All three of these minority "peace" movements offer the possibility of revising the expectations and behavior, though not yet the dominant tone, of three segments of the next generation of

117

Americans. Needless to say, these minority movements, which in turn subdivide, will continue to have varied images of the American mission and approaches to these policy ends, reflecting their very different social positions and experiences. The new class movements for peace especially reflect wide diversity in stated goals and action emphases.

Among the new class there has been an efflorescence of movements in the past dozen years. These have had different ways of expressing themselves and varied institutional bases. Within the new class one can distinguish: the *reform* movement of the Stevensonians who subsequently created organizations of reform Democrats in New York and California and a few other places; the postwar *peace* movement in the narrow sense, made up overwhelmingly of new class people, traditionally bipartisan; and the *student* movements, whose people have been typically the children of the new class and thus themselves the new class from birth, acting differently from the first generation of the new class. These various new class movements typically provide the troops for what we think of as the peace organizations. Yet we must keep in mind the overclass and underclass kinds of peace movements, neither of which looks like the usual peace organization.

2. FOUR MAJOR MODES OF PEACE ACTION

There are several kinds of action being undertaken by people in the United States, frequently specifically oriented to the Vietnam War and to a lesser extent more generally oriented to the war problem as a whole. This paper concentrates on four modes of action that now have major significance:

1. The use of power through the electoral process to change the government that carries on a foreign policy;

2. The building of a new base of community organization capable of transforming a very considerable part of the American social structure, aimed at changing the society that creates foreign policy;

3. Standing in the way of the government that carries on a foreign policy, by direct action and resistance, such civil dis-

obedience assuming that when a government is forced to behave differently towards its own people, it will have to change its overseas behavior;

4. Transnational modes of action, in which chunks of people from one country act jointly with chunks of people in other countries, moving together *around* or *against* governments and organized (as are the churches) to stand outside any given nation and resist the self-serving policies of a particular government or allied governments.

A. ELECTORAL POLITICS

At this point, elections to change the government—that is, the use of the electoral machinery to change the people who carry on the foreign policy of the United States and therefore to change the foreign policy, to end the war in Vietnam, and to undertake a peace-oriented foreign policy—electoral peace activities focus around different versions of a "dump-Johnson" movement. There is the version that says it is possible to eliminate Johnson as the candidate of the Democratic Party in 1968. There is the version that assumes Johnson's renomination but says it is possible for the Republican Party to nominate a peace-oriented candidate and to elect him. There is the version that says that one or the other of those might conceivably happen but is unlikely. Persons of this persuasion argue that even if the Republicans nominate a nonpeace nonwar candidate, it would be important to diselect Johnson. Therefore, the best way to do that would be to create a third party that was clearly a peace party which people could vote for, thereby subtracting votes from the Democrats and electing the Republican even if he were not a clear peace candidate.

Several groups of people are focusing on how to "dump" President Johnson in 1968 so as to change the foreign policy of the United States. They tend to be disillusioned liberal Democrats. There seem to be some disillusioned moderate Republicans who have the same idea, but primarily because they are suddenly discovering that there are hundreds and hundreds of thousands of disillusioned Democrats whose votes are up for

119

grabs, and open to a peace platform. Within the party there are also some extremely distressed Republicans who have become distressed because they think that it is necessary to make peace in Vietnam and neither the Dirksen line nor the Johnson line, which are the same line, can do that. In both parties there are ambiguous signals of a turn in direction towards making peace in Vietnam.

Now electoral peace action comes mostly from new class people, from reform Democrats, moderate Republicans, from the peace movement in the narrower sense, and perhaps in some part from the churches. It does not come from the students, nor from the New Politics group. Some of them are certainly interested in electoral politics, but for another reason discussed below.

While this is mostly a new class phenomenon, as you would expect, it has important allies in the establishment peace movement, including some prominent members of Congress. The foreign policy "establishment" is comprised of a select but somewhat variable group of influentials with leadership roles in international corporations, foundations, universities, and key Federal government posts. One of their qualifications is that they have been in such positions of influence, or rotated chairs, for a number of years (some for more than twenty-five years). An establishment peace movement oriented to changing the board of foreign policy directors is growing for two very serious reasons.

One is the awareness of part of the establishment—still a minority—that it is simply impossible to use modern weaponry to win political victories. The Cuban missile crisis was a major lesson in the knowledge that once war has hypertrophied, the victories you win are absolutely minimal despite the taking of overwhelming risks. Cuba taught this lesson because traditionally, with three to one military superiority in the most dreadful weapons in history, the United States should have been able to demand and get the total transformation of Cuban society or the Soviet posture. But in fact, as a result of the Cuban missile crisis little changed—Cuba did not change her social system nor Russia her posture. What happened in the missile crisis was only Russia's removal of about forty missiles from the island of Cuba, a kind of minimal marginal reduction of Soviet firepower taken as a whole. Minimal results were gained for an over-whelming risk—the risk of thermonuclear war. After that, peo-ple began uneasily to decide that overwhelming superiority in thermonuclear weapons didn't matter because it didn't work to win what it was supposed to.

Now in Vietnam, people are uneasily beginning to discover that somehow even "conventional" superiority doesn't work to win political ends. It didn't work very well in Korea to win political ends; it won a minimal political end: a stalemate. It did not change the situation in Korea that had stood before the conventional fight. The attempted counter-guerrilla war in Viet-nam clearly failed, and the result was to try something like conventional warfare which is in the process of failing.

Pondering these events of the '60s, a chunk of the Establish-ment—only a minority chunk, but growing—comes to the conclusion that there is something wrong with that foreign-policy technique. Without revising long-term ends, those who influence the managers, or are themselves managers of the for-eign-policy machinery, begin to search for some other sets of means. They begin to cast about for a way to curtail fruitless military means in particular. Obviously, the other response to discovering that the means aren't working is to say that they haven't been used big enough, and that response has happened too, as you know. But what's interesting is that suddenly there is a major increase in the group that scratches its head and comes to the conclusion that there is no point in magnifying present means, because United States military power is really overwhelming already, and if present means were going to work they would have worked already. Therefore, something must be basically wrong with the means and we had better use some-thing else. It doesn't mean that these people give up their foreign policy goals. They may end up using money instead of guns to dominate, but some are looking for new means. Vietnam cer-tainly accelerates any strains among the overclass over the value of the war-making system.

The other impact on the establishment is tied to the under-class and to some extent the new class. For the first time in the twentieth century, the foreign-policy managers discover that war doesn't unite the country but divides it, and they find themselves in an absolutely remarkable political box. In oversimplified terms, one might say that in the twentieth century the American establishment has always used the Democratic Party to bring about the minimal change necessary to keep it and American society going, when it looked as if it were in serious trouble. The overclass has always used the Republican Party to end a war, or to put things back together after one, and to keep the social system going on course with themselves in happy control of it, under normal circumstances. Then when that happy operation gets out of kilter, perhaps because it's too happy and they are getting too fat, they then use the Democratic Party to put things back in shape again.

The overclass holders of public and private resources now find themselves in the absolutely remarkable political situation that at one and the same time they have to do some kind of social reform inside the United States, and end a major war. Now you can't do them both at the same time with either of the parties. Somehow they got themselves in the box where the Democratic Party, which ought to have been able to make the social reforms, *reforms* only, necessary to keep the ghetto quiet, is not able to do so because it is carrying on a war. The Republican Party which might be able to end the war, is normally not equipped to carry on social reforms in the United States. It is not set up to do that; it is set up *not* to do social reform.

One can imagine a situation where overclass people throw their weight behind candidates who might end the war and then cannot do the social reform, which would leave matters desperate at home. That terrible political dilemma is cracking the overclass apart, as some choose the one necessity and others choose the other necessity. They are trying desperately, given the rebellions at home, the disaffection of a big chunk of the new class, and so forth, to move in the direction of ending the war so as to make social reform possible, and evidently they will then try to cope with how on earth they are going to get reform once they have made it possible. Some members of the Establishment obviously are interested in changing the people who actually run the government and they are therefore tying themselves cautiously to those in the new class who are interested in using elections for that same purpose.

Distinct from electoral politics, but closely related to it, is lobbying to influence the policy makers. Especially when it comes to the politics of war and peace, lobbying groups have little impact if they cannot do something at the next election. Lobbying efforts should be included in the topography, but with an asterisk next to them saying "alone ineffective." They are useful for some purposes. They are useful as support for the committed. If a congressman is opposed to the war and he wants to know what to keep saying day after day after day, it is useful for the FCNL (Friends Committee on National Legislation) to feed him material that makes up speeches, but a lobby does not change his mind by providing him that material. It may be that a few minds get changed among the legislative assistants, and that can be important in the long run, but even that won't be important unless the congressman sees how to let it be important—that is, sees how he can afford to move politically.

Lobbying sometimes encourages a congressman to take a new step that he has not made before, especially if the lobbying group has an increment of power back home; congressmen are very conscious of this. It is hard to influence them to make that next step if they know there is nothing to back them up at home. They don't *want* to be persuaded until they feel that they won't be destroyed if they *are* persuaded.

I can imagine a case, and I even suspect it is not wholly imaginary but is actually happening. Congressmen who were baffled by the strange impact the war was having on the budget, and therefore on the economy, were baffled in the sense that for a while they didn't know how the war was having that impact. There were very peculiar things going on in the American economy; and there was also the war. The Administration was obscuring the amount of money that the war was costing, misleading people about the impact of the war on the financial structure. It took some peace people to plot out the factual evidence; it took some peace people to sit down with the Congressmen and say, "Now this is the way the war is creating that, and when you get so upset about this over here you had better understand that the war is why it is happening." Some Congressmen had not made such connections, but once they were made, the impetus already existed for them to be upset about the result.

123

When they could explain to their people the reason for that result, then they were much more likely to be distressed about the war. There are moments when technical information, even new ideas which offer a Congressman a way around what he thought was a dilemma, may give him an attitude he did not have before. Yet, given equal inputs of energy, electoral peace action seems more effective than lobbying.

There is one undeveloped aspect to the role of the existing peace lobbies. Let us take the Friends Committee on National Legislation, which as lobbies go—especially lobbies with no power behind them—is pretty good. The FCNL's *Washington Newsletter,* which goes out to people across the country, is very useful in discussing the bills before Congress and what might be said about them. Testimony is presented, which is very smart testimony, and Congressmen say that they know the FCNL does not lie, they trust its facts. But what the FCNL does not do is try to build a base back home. It does a few things that might contribute to that. For instance, it sends out its own version of the roll-call countdown, like 60 % good, 40 % bad, which is useful to people who are considering whether to support a man for re-election. It does not do what I would regard as being enormously important to do, that is, just as it reports the box score of how a Congressman voted, it might report the real political bases he has, so that local groups know how to cope with him. Where are his sources of contributions, what is his ethnic base in his district, what other ethnic bases are there in his district? That sort of information would offer a real chance for people back home to build an opposition to or support for him, or bring power to bear on him.

B. COMMUNITY ORGANIZATION

The second major form of action looks for community organization to change very considerably the shape of American society and, as a sidelight, to change its foreign policy. This comes from that group of people which is convinced that in a sense the war is not an accidental mistake by the American overclass, or if it was, the only way to prevent similar mistakes in the future is to get rid of the overclass that can make such mistakes. They are convinced that the only way to have a peaceful foreign policy is to change American society.

The world-conscious community organizers tend to be the radical elements of the new class movements, that is, the students especially, and some of the people in the underclass. Increasingly both groups are concluding from the depressing experience of the last three years that reasonable debate about foreign policy brings very limited results. Many of them thought the war was just a mistake and if you set people straight, you would stop it. If you held a teach-in and explained very carefully how it was a mistake, then they would end it. When public criticism of the Vietnam policy made no discernible impact, some groups tried to build other kinds of pressure and power and it still made little difference. Then they became convinced that there were really very basic changes necessary in American political structure.

For example, one of the reasons the war could be initiated the way it was is that a very large number of Americans—not just the underclass—have no power in reality to say what goes on in the society, and that when they do try to say it, at best the society pats them on the head and says, "It's really great you're dissenting," and goes right on doing what it was doing before. That means dissenters don't have power, because if they had power they could change the way the society acts. Therefore, many of these people have decided the best thing to do is to build power, which means to organize, which means to put people together with a cohesive voice. The first lesson they learned was that isolated citizens are quite powerless; the second was that you can never build power if you think you have it already.

So the first message of the radicals of the new class and the underclass is, "You are powerless and you must get together to build power." This signals the building of some very nitty-gritty things at the base of American society. They are trying to organize the ghetto, or the middle-class neighborhood, or some of the professions to be against the war and to stand together to take certain kinds of action against the war.

These organizers are quite eclectic about what kinds of behavior do the organizing. Usually they organize direct pressure against the control systems that afflict people—such as a watch-your-local-police group, or a welfare rights organization, or a tenants union. Sometimes they see massive sit-ins as a way to organize people—radicalize them, show them that the police are not there to protect them but to beat them up whenever the government is challenged, as happened in Los Angeles when people tried to picket the President's speech there in June 1967.

Or, they may decide that an election is the best way to organize people because it energizes people around a given issue. If you have a candidate who expresses an issue effectively, you not only educate people but you build an ongoing network of contact. Result: an organization. People come together who trust one another, like one another, know one another, and are ready to work together, and that is an organization. Suddenly you have power if you do that, even if you lose the election. So these people frequently are interested in elections to build a base, not elections to change the government, except ultimately. The new politics people, for instance in Berkeley, are much more oriented to organizing semi-permanent groups than they are to an election that would change the Administration. For instance, in Chicago, at the new politics convention, where some people were talking about a national ticket for President because they wanted to defeat Lyndon Johnson, the California new politics people were talking about it because they wanted to organize California. Since many people believed a national ticket would drain energies away from most areas, a pluralistic approach emerged. All right, why don't you have your ticket in California, but don't bother us in D.C. or Connecticut or somewhere where there are other things that need doing.

There has also been talk about trying to organize neighborhoods around the third mode of action that I will take up shortly —resistance and direct action of various kinds. For instance, in the 49th ward of Chicago there is now beginning a campaign for that ward to secede from the taxes that support the war; that is, to try to organize tax refusal not on an individual conscience basis, but to have the whole neighborhood refuse, and put the money into neighborhood improvement through a *de facto* neighborhood government which tries to act as if the war did not exist for it, and which tries to build things the neighborhood desperately needs that it could never build or control before. Or—not quite so radical a departure—there is interest among peace movement people about trying to create a peace-and-freedom neighborhood budget. Begin with the assumption of twenty-five billion dollars going to the war. Translate that into the amount of money it would mean in a given place if all that money were devoted to social investment (not just given back in tax reductions that produce bigger tail fins or more automated factories). Put into social investment, what would that money mean for a given area? The neighborhood works out the way they would spend that amount of money, thereby creating a demand that the war end and that the money be made available. I did a little arithmetic for the neighborhood I come from in Washington, the neighborhood called Adams-Morgan, which has a community council which is maybe 40% of the way towards being a legitimate democratic institution. Adams-Morgan has about twenty-five thousand people in it. Assuming the war costs at least twenty-five billion dollars a year, and assuming that you apportion that money equally, ignoring disparities in per capita income of some parts of the country against other parts, and assuming that you give it to neighborhood institutions (cities having big chunks of money already), what are the annual resources? It means that the Adams-Morgan council would have three-million dollars a year to spend as it saw fit—on the schools, on a guaranteed annual income for the neighborhood, or on incredible things—I mean three-million dollars. The chairman of the council could not believe it, but she could imagine using it. The council's budget now—its organizing budget plus its program budget—is somewhere around forty-thousand dollars. So people are talking about building organizations at a neighborhood level where people can really imagine what the resources could be. Twenty-five billion dollars a year doesn't mean a thing —it might just as well be zero. None of us can know what to do with twenty-five billion dollars or what the country would do, but a local community organization can imagine what it could do with three million dollars. (Even if half that sum were factored out for nonmilitary use overseas, the remaining one and a half million dollars now used to plow up Vietnam would be a fabulous neighborhood resource.)

As efforts at community organization proceed, three groups of people bear watching. Obviously, indigenous leaders in underclass ghettos are the central figures in attempts to redirect American resources from the war. They have become more articulate about this recently, drawing connections between the Vietnam war and the needs of their own people. They are asking two pointed questions. "Why should Black people kill their dark-skinned brothers and be killed by them?" "Why doesn't the power structure make it possible to spend the money here?" Those question will be asked with louder volume as time goes on.

Two groups of the new class are also in transition. The newest generation of national leaders among students, for example, Students for a Democratic Society, is interested in community organization, avoiding electoral politics. Electoral politics are viewed by them as a means to stimulate underclass organization of power with a voice. Among the middle class they propose, and are beginning to try, organization in association with work, apart from neighborhood or party. Work-place organizing may lead to Teachers for a Democratic Society, Social Workers for a Democratic Society, and so forth. They are asking what it means to be radical in the professions. They challenge the assumption that electoral politics is more important in the process of social change.

Many of the candidates for radicalization are older, liberal new-class people, who might be described as despairing Stevensonians. These persons have attempted to step away from merely quiet service in corporate systems. They are organized in reform groups, and many of them have taken a very strong anti-war position, but not an anti-society position. Most of them have not decided that we need to change American society in large measure in order to end the war or such wars. Two or three years ago, indeed, many of these liberals thought that the United States needed only to solve the race question and to achieve disarmament, and that we were on the track towards both goals. Those were the two last major social problems. Now they look around three years later and they realize that seven and one half years of the most heroic kind of social action by the Black community has hardly changed the situation. On many of the real questions Black Americans are no better off. Why has all that energy produced so little in results, if all that was needed was the last finishing touches on civil rights? And they look at America as of the election of 1964, when the Administration had reduced the military budget, and was talking world disarmament. Why since then has the United States spent three years pouring fire and shell onto one of the smaller, weaker, and poorer countries in the world? So much for disarmament. I think some liberals are on the verge of concluding that they can't any longer say, "All that needs doing is the fulfillment of those two important social demands." They haven't boiled over yet, but they are simmering. Some of them may be ready to swing free.

C. DIRECT RESISTANCE

The third kind of approach to peace action—direct action and resistance—comes from the most radical element of the society, both the radical elements of the underclass and from the new class, especially university students and teachers, some churchmen and church peace organizations, and perhaps new politics people. Resistance and direct action mean refusal to participate in the draft, refusal to participate in the tax system insofar as it goes for war, direct blockage of various war institutions such as induction centers and napalm plants, and also resistance to the government as a whole.

In 1967, acts of total resistance occurred in the ghettos, specifically in Newark and Detroit. Although it may seem to stretch logic, it helps to ponder the Newark and Detroit rebellions as a kind of peace movement. In my opinion, the single most effective action anyone took in 1967 towards ending the war in Vietnam was the Detroit rebellion. That, for instance, was what really pushed Senator Thruston Morton, more than the Spring Mobilization's putting 400,000 people in the streets of New York and San Francisco last April. The ghetto rebellion may have involved fewer than three or four hundred thousand people in the streets, but they were doing a great deal more

129

troublesome things than the people at the Spring Mobilization. Although part of the response of the establishment has been to suppress, to pass anti-riot legislation, part of the response has been, "My God, we cannot carry on America with that going on, and therefore we have to end the war in order to be able to cope with it." For that reason, we had better think about the Black rebellions as one form of peace movement, whether we like them as a form of peace movement or not. (Obviously there are all kinds of ethical choices about these things. Some of us don't like the establishment manipulation of the Republican nomination as a way to win peace, but we recognize it as a peace movement of a special kind.)

Resistance, direct action, what is that coming to mean? It is coming to mean draft resistance, with students trying to work out a sense of obligation to refuse to be drafted whether or not they have II-S or C.O. status (student deferment or conscientious objector). Some of them puzzle with the fact that they have II-S status, and therefore wouldn't be drafted, but they consider themselves draft resisters anyway, because they wouldn't go in any case. What does that mean they should do with their time and energy? Many of them feel committed to organize rather than study, and some may therefore lose their II-S's and find themselves resisting for real. Others have refused to register or have returned their draft cards or burned them. Still others have found asylum in Canada. A few servicemen have dropped out of the Army, either by requesting C.O. status (though most such have been refused) or by going A.W.O.L. (and deserters are finding asylum in Sweden and France). Intellectuals and clergymen have offered sanctuary, money, and other kinds of help to draft resisters and are increasingly trying to share their resistance by violating the law against counseling or abetting draft resistance.

Tax refusal is also building up around the country. People are discovering new techniques like Federal telephone tax refusal, which puts a fantastic burden on the government to collect—the telephone tax is so small that to collect it would cost more than the tax itself. This can be arranged without getting your telephone service turned off and without straining relations with the telephone company, if you simply inform them what you are doing and why.

130

Some people are thinking about direct blockage: not only withdrawal, not only refusing a tax, or refusing to serve, but attempting to block ongoing institutions like munitions plants and induction centers. These people say: "We won't go and it's immoral to send other people. Therefore we're going to try to block operation of the induction center." Or, "It's immoral to use napalm so we won't let you manufacture it." I suggested in *The Christian Century* that clergymen should take crosses and block napalm plants, and force the government to desecrate the cross in order to carry on the war, which is what it is doing in basic fact anyway, but force them to do it in symbolic, visible reality as well. I got a number of warm responses, and no letters saying you're out of your mind, you're unpatriotic. But no action —yet.

Clearly the most remarkable single example of direct resistance has been the siege of the Pentagon on October 21–22, 1967. That action was in some ways the firmest challenge to the moral and legal authority of the government since South Carolina fired on Fort Sumter. And it was done chiefly by nonviolence. Despite the press reports, I can testify that most of the "invasion" was done gently, that an overwhelming proportion of the violence was initiated by United States marshals against seated demonstrators and was frequently brutal and sadistic, that when a few demonstrators responded to such brutality by throwing things at the troops the crowd firmly stopped them, and that over and over the crowd talked and acted towards the troops not as enemies but as brothers to be persuaded: all within a context of total rejection of the legitimacy of the government.

Of course, difficult moral choices and judgments cluster around every attempt at direct resistance and civil disobedience. When is the disorder creative and when is it mere anarchy? The daily press is not very helpful in sorting out the moral and institutional issues at stake. But serious writing is available and church assemblies have made a few statements that members should ponder.

One adopts civil disobedience only as a last resort in cases where one is very clear that the moral law or the written law is being violated. There is a treaty ratified by the United States called the Geneva Conventions of 1949 which specifies a series

131

of acts which are war crimes. There is an international obligation agreed to by the United States at Nuremberg and underlined at Geneva that individuals ordered to commit war crimes have a positive duty not only to avoid them but, in certain circumstances, they have a positive duty to prevent them from being done. Many of the war crimes listed in the Geneva Conventions of 1949 are being violated by the United States in Vietnam.

It is very hard for reasonable people to get together and look at the facts and not agree that they are being violated. Under those circumstances, even under American domestic law, if there were some way to believe that it could be enforced against the President, the Cabinet, and the Congress, the activities the United States is now carrying on in Vietnam would be punishable by imprisonment. Therefore, if it is a crime to do those things, one can come to the conclusion that it is no crime to refuse to do them or to try to prevent their being done. Secondly, whatever the Geneva Conventions of 1949 tried to codify, one still has the obligation to make a moral judgment. That is the obligation of religious people all the time.

It is among the weightiest of decisions to decide when to disobey orders that have been given the façade of legitimacy and law by the constituted authorities, especially in a society where the legitimacy seems to be founded upon the democratic decision-making process. Yet it is difficult to discern a democratic decision-making process in the United States today on the issues of foreign policy and especially the war in Vietnam. Notice, for example, that in the 1964 election the American people thought they had a clear choice between war and peace in Vietnam, voted for peace, and within six months had their decision totally reversed. Nevertheless, even assuming that at least 51 % of the American public had deliberately, consciously, knowingly voted to commit war crimes in Vietnam, men of faith would still have the obligation to decide whether they can participate or must resist.

Action for peace invariably meets the ingrained assumption that the war system works and the government should be obeyed, *especially* when it goes to war, rather than being changed or resisted. One still bumps into the people who say, "The President has all the facts; therefore you critics must be wrong." That is simply a variation of the theme that the government must be obeyed no matter what. This concept of governmental authority is now awash, even among those who haven't yet decided to resist it by means of civil disobedience.

D. TRANSNATIONAL ACTION

Fourth, a growing number of people have opportunities for transnational action. The term "transnational" does not mean government-to-government action, which is "international." Nor does it mean "the whole people to the whole people," in fuzzy communication. Transnational action involves groups of people across national boundaries, whether through permanent organizations or *ad hoc* movements. The building of an "international" labor movement was in fact a transnational action. The building of a student movement across national boundaries is a transnational action, when done by the students themselves. (Two such movements of the last generation looked as if they were transnational. One was in fact clearly international—the eastern bloc's International Union of Students, which was clearly sponsored and dictated to by a set of governments; and the other, the International Student Conference, which people thought was transnational and created by the student movements themselves, turned out after all to have been founded by several national governments and dominated by one of them—our own, through the CIA.)

The churches are perhaps the best-developed transnational organizations, as weak as they are in standing up to national governments. World Council of Churches reactions and the efforts of Pope Paul concerning the war in Vietnam indicate the potential for transnational organizations to stand outside any given nation and to resist in part some of its foreign policy behavior. The transnational role of the church could be a great deal stronger than it is. For example, a world Protestant-Catholic commission could be established to examine the justice of warfare in Vietnam. Its report could have enormous weight. Or a transnational group of clergymen could physically intervene against the bombing of North Vietnam. Or the illegal Quaker

133

efforts to send medical supplies to Hanoi could be taken up by many churches, and the laws of most governments against aiding "the enemy" in such ways could be broken by the churches until it was firmly established that the commitment to mankind transcends even war.

A related kind of transnational peace action would be to establish a free-lance academy of peace keepers who are trained to combine the functions of policeman, conciliator, and developer.

Under certain circumstances, the alumni could be directed by the general board of this academy to act in an international crisis, even if the United Nations or other international organizations were unprepared for that. It would be hoped that independent peace keepers would get into trouble and the trouble would press the world community to decide how to exert control over the emergence of a cadre of peace keepers. Given the present lack of consensus about world law and institutions, and the probability that any world laws adopted by the powerful nations in the next generation will be unjust to the poor nations, the most hopeful interim peace-keeping goal is international competition by nonmilitary means, checked and moderated by the growing power of transnational institutions.

Transnational action is the longest range, the least likely to bring about immediate change, less likely even than community organization intended to transform American society. Yet transnational action offers the longest range major hope that not only this particular war or that particular war, but all war, can be abolished. Transnational action challenges the pretentious sovereignty of national governments, so that they no longer command every loyalty of most of their people. If it comes to a head-on clash between one's loyalty to an organization that inspires professional or religious commitment and the command of one's territorial national government, members of transnational organizations are more likely to opt out of the situation than to obey automatically their national government. That is one of the most important possible ingredients—not the only one by any means—of a changing world that just cannot carry on the war system.

15
Towards a Democratic Futurism

When the Foreign Policy Association celebrated its fifty years of history last fall in a New York Hilton dinner chaired by Charlie "Goldfinger" Engelhard and addressed by Dean Rusk, the movement met the dinner with a quasi-military assault. Frightened that it might be losing the generation that will guide the next 50 years, FPA turned to a convocation it was planning on the year 2018, as the appropriate moment to invite the movement to negotiate. Did not the mysterious young, after all, believe at least in imagining the future?

Well, they do and they don't. It depends on how, by whom, and for what—in short, on the politics of the imagining. And this the FPA could never grasp, for it was sunk so deep in the assumptions of its own politics that it could not believe they were political at all—just "neutral education." So it spent over $150,-000 on a convocation at the New York Hilton, May 27–29, 1968, that turned off hundreds more of the younger generation.

The FPA's recipe for a disaster:

1. Invite 500 people over 35 years old and 500 under (including about 50 of the more intellectual New Left and another 50 new-liberal leaders—such as Peace Corps returned volunteers and insurgent Pennsylvania assemblymen).

2. Circulate a dreadful little book of 13 chapters by such people as Ithiel de Sola Pool (who takes public-opinion surveys on how much the Vietnamese love Americans); Herman Kahn (on economics this year), and Najeeb Halaby (senior vice-president of Panam, writing on transportation), each celebrating some new "inevitable" gadget and deducing all social "change" —that is; no major change at all—from a kind of gadgetary determinism.

3. Invite 22 speakers, of whom the only one under 35 is Bill

Moyers—whose power base and sense of life scarcely come from the youth.

4. Have the meeting chaired by a colorless ex-professor (and State Department, of course, consultant) who trembles at the sight of a beard, tells jokes nobody laughs at, and thinks letting John Kenneth Galbraith speak is a concession to the New Left.

Without the radicals this would simply have been the recipe for a crashing bore. But they translated yawns into irreverent rebellion, forced some of their number to be accepted as commentators and speakers, held some unauthorized teach-ins, and laid bare to a large number of liberals, moderates, and FPA staff both how biased and how boring the FPA was.

The radicals tried to make a more basic point: not simply that radicals should have been invited to speak, but that even if they had been, no convocation of the kind FPA put together could have led to a democratic futurism. Not chiefly because of its content—the pro-military views of almost all the speakers, the assumption that technological development would necessarily follow precisely the same lines it had over the past 50 years (as if these were "natural" rather than politically chosen and politically changeable), the focus on how economic development could be done by the rich for (maybe) the poor, instead of by the poor for themselves. Much more crucial was the very process of the convocation: bringing the future "leaders" of America together to share the delights of contemplating their future leadership. The notion that the future of America should be constructed by the people of America—school teachers, welfare mothers, auto workers, shopkeepers, high-school dropouts—would have dictated quite a different format.

The format FPA adopted was closely connected with the emergence in the last few years of a "profession" of the study of the future. In the American Academy of Arts and Sciences, there is a Commission on the Year 2000, headed by Daniel Bell of Columbia University. (He was a major figure at the Hilton.) The Commission very much regarded itself as a panel of the priesthood: to whom the mysteries were revealed and who could guide the people, but would not open those mysteries to the people. (When one member of the Commission proposed inviting a number of young people to join it on the ground that they might actually live till the year 2000, he was told that mere youth could not make them experts—and only experts could do the requisite planning.)

In the RAND Corporation, there has grown out of concern with the future of military strategy a group with a wider interest in the future of American policy generally; but that interest remains oriented to the group of people that run the government of the United States and is still based on the assumption that this need not, could not, ought not, be in any sense the property of the American public. (The RAND group helped bring into being an Institute on the Future which opened its doors on Carnegie and Ford Foundation grants.)

The new élite futurologists of course deny that élitism is a problem at all, saying that just as astronomy is a matter for the professional, so the study of the future has to be. These experts —and their overseas analogues like the *Futuribles* group in France—relay their "findings" to the public through books, pamphlets, top-down conferences, and so on. And usually they take the "public" to mean a somewhat larger circle of experts, administrations, and politicians. Very few of the élite futurists even respond to a challenge that is democratically couched: Who does the future belong to? Is it indeed a subject like astronomy, or something quite different in that the future of the world presumably belongs to all the people of the world—who should therefore understand and decide it?

One possible response of democrats to the emergence of this highly professionalized, élitist study of the future is to shrug it off, saying that this makes little difference; that politics comes from quite different sources—not from intellectual analysis of what might be done and should be done, either on the part of the haves or the have-nots, but from much more visceral responses of people to the place they hold in society and the way that society is treating them: in short, that change comes from revulsion and anger at the present, so far as the excluded are concerned, and from an urgent desire to protect their holdings, on the part of the powerful.

That may well be true; but it does not gainsay the old fact

137

that knowledge is power, and that in a super-industrial (some people have even said a "post-industrial") society, knowledge of the future is enormous power and ignorance of the future may prevent one from feeling revulsion and anger until it is too late. Decisions on research and development of weapon systems made today will affect what the world looks like twenty years from now. They will affect, for example, whether it is even *possible* to achieve a disarmed world twenty years hence. Decisions on seemingly less crucial matters like the supersonic transport will affect the way our cities develop ten years hence. And very few people know this—only the experts with an "interest" in the matter, with an established political or economic interest which they already know about. The rest of the public is not ready to worry, not trained to worry; it won't get angry about sonic booms till the SST's are already there, and that will be too late. In an era of very swift technological change, it has to be possible for the whole public to be able to understand the possible futures confronting their society 20, 25, 30 years from now, in order to be able to insist on the decisions to be made now that would enable the kind of society to emerge 20 or 30 years from now that they want.

In response to these conflicting values and interests of the public and private good, there have emerged various and conflicting styles of futurism. At the First International Future Research Congress, held in September 1967, in Oslo, the futurists divided into these groups. One might be called the techno-planners—concerned chiefly with technological forecasting. They had frequently been involved in systems-analysis kinds of work; they saw the future as buildable through governments and similar large-scale institutions with very considerable power. Most of these people were from the United States; many of them came out of the RAND Corporation or similar kinds of institutions. And they were vigorously putting forward their images of how one might construct pieces of the twenty-first century, and describing ways in which they have worked with governments in the super-industrial or in the underdeveloped world, to try to construct those pieces. For them, "planning" was clearly a way of helping those who now hold power to know what they must do in order to keep holding power thirty or fifty years hence.

What must they change, where should they beat a strategic retreat, what new organizations and technologies should they invent, when can they hold the line?

The second major group at Oslo might be called the humanist social democrats. They included both a great number of the western Europeans and a great number of the eastern Europeans, plus a couple of Americans. They were typically in their mid-50s, about a decade older than the techno-planners. They were quite distressed at technocratic planning. The eastern Europeans tended to be very fearful of the way it had gone in eastern Europe, for example. They tended to be very critical of the way central planning had operated in the twenty years from 1946 or '47 until fairly recently; and were concerned about the ignoring of human values that had resulted from pressure from a central planning source for technological advance and swift economic development. They tended to see the western, especially American, technocrats as very similar to the state planners with whom they'd had to cope in Poland and Czechoslovakia. And they feared that human values would similarly get lost. There was considerable horror, for example, over an attempt to plan a 700 million megalopolis on the Bay of Bengal for the middle of the twenty-first century—the second group feeling horrified that this could not possibly be a *human* social system and that planning it and getting the Indian government to begin building it was the same kind of process that they had gone through in eastern Europe. They were very frightened of that, and most of the western Europeans agreed with them.

In reaction against the "expert" orientation of the élitist technological planners, the social democrats at their best have tried to move one step beyond "planning" towards teaching the general public the art of thinking in a 30-to-40 year span. For example, the discussions of the "Mankind 2000" project, involving an international group of scholars, centering in Western Europe and Britain but including some Americans and East Europeans, have focused on how to involve large numbers of the public in planning the future. Robert Jungk of the Mankind 2000 group has suggested a permanent (perhaps mobile) exposition on the future, in which larger numbers of visitors than those usually oriented to books would be exposed to vivid exhibitions of the possible social realities of the future. Charles Osgood of the Mankind 2000 group is exploring, through Project PLATO at the University of Illinois, the possibilities of using computer and teaching machine technology to make available complex sets of branching choices, leading to various futures, so that participants could play through certain choices in the present to see how they might open up and close off various possible futures.

Both of these experimental efforts move in the direction of involving large sections of the public in future-thinking, but both still present the public with *faits accomplis* and leave little room for the invention of new forms or parts of the future, on the local and personal levels, that would mesh with large-scale change and make it viable.

Finally, there was at Oslo a third group, made up of several young North Americans and several young western Europeans, especially a couple of Englishmen and some Scandinavians— typically in their early thirties. They might be called the participatory futurists. They were equally distressed by top-down technocratic planning and by what many of them felt was a kind of literary fuzziness in the humanist social democrats. They criticized the social democrats from the standpoint that they were not able to make anything real out of their fears or their hopes, and that the literary and philosophical musings with which they seemed to confront top-down planning, whether the Eastern or Western variety, was not an effective way of building the kind of future which they seemed to want to build.

The typical methodology of this third group of people could be called one of "creative disorder": that is, attempting to project a decent and workable vision of the future over a one-generation-hence time period, *and then attempting to build chunks of that future in the present.* But not to build them with the help of presently powerful institutions; to build them from the bottom, without the permission of the powerful and often against the laws or the mores of the present "order".

Some of the participatory futurists were working on such unorthodox projects, chunks of a possible future, as neighborhood-level quasi-governments in metropolitan centers—democratically run and oriented partly to such traditional issues as schools or housing, but also involved in imagining alternative futures for the neighborhood. Others at Oslo were working on putting together transnational groups of scholars and students interested in projecting visions of world order—which those groups of people, by their very existence and action as transnational bodies, would help to bring into existence.

And the methodology of this third group was, therefore, quite different from the methodology of both of the first two. They did not tend to do any technological forecasting; most of them were not technologically trained; and they were deeply skeptical about involvement with governments as the way of bringing about a decent future.

At the New York Hilton, it became clear the Foreign Policy Association had never imagined any kind of futurists but the first: the élite, technologically oriented "planners." The conference was intended to tell the future second-level leaders of America what to plan for. The shock of confrontation with the movement came from the movement's demand for participatory futurism. And though the movement was not yet ready to specify how to go about *doing* participatory futurism, it was ready to draw upon its own experience. Although the movement has been unwilling to develop detailed images of what the future decent society might look like, it has in a very narrow and *ad hoc* way (a way that we should recognize, mull over, and deliberately turn into a conscious method) been focusing on images of the future. The neatest case is the sit-ins, where the civil rights movement said:

> Our desirable-achievable future is that we want to be able to eat in integrated restaurants. We will not petition legislatures to require integration, we will not petition the owners of the restaurants to integrate, *we will simply create the future*. That is, *we* will integrate the restaurants, and it will rest upon those who have the power of law and the power of ownership in their hands, to decide how to respond to that creation. So we will build *now* what it is we want to exist in the future, and the powerful will have to react to that.

141

They will have to let us build it, or punish us for trying. If they punish us, we believe we can build support around that vision of the future, and can therefore mobilize even more people into action to achieve it.

So also the draft-resistance movement, whose imagined future was one without conscription; and the Quaker medical-aid-to-North-Vietnam program, whose imagined future was one where national enmities and even boundaries had dissolved in the face of need; and the student-power movement, whose imagined future was one where students always had access to Administration files because they shared control over the Administration.

All these efforts assume the creation of strains and tensions between the imagined future and the existing present. Creating and judging the strain is crucial. If it is not done well, the possibilities are these: One might create something so utterly out of relation with the present, and so challenging to it, that it is smashed immediately beyond repair, in which case one is unlikely to have created much change. On the other hand, one can import into the present something so irrelevant that it is simply encapsulated and allowed to go its own way without creating any tension, and therefore any change at all. Both those poles have to be avoided if one can, and one way to avoid them is simply to keep experimenting and to discover at what point one is neither smashed nor ignored, but creates enough change to move the society. *That* is creative disorder; disorder because it obeys the "law and order" of some more or less distant future, and is therefore likely to be "unlawful" or "disorderly" by the standards of the present.

One who uses this approach should not expect that his picture of the future will be achieved. That is, one does not expect that sitting in 1967, one can draw a 1999 which world society will, in fact, be like in 1999. We must expect exactly the opposite: that along the way the process of imagination and creation will lead one to change his imagination. If all goes well, the process will engage wholly new people in imagining the future who do not now imagine it, and by doing that will engage them in creation of a kind of future which was not imagined by the ones who began the process. That is one of the major goals, and therefore one should expect to move in the direction of it; one should expect perhaps to move in some quite different direction after moving part way, but never *to* it. And indeed, it might be wise to set a deadline, a five or ten-year deadline, at the end of which we throw the old image away and start over again. In a sense this is like the process of science at its best: hypothesis, experiment, new hypothesis—always knowing that no theory is "the truth," but only a useful and beautiful way of understanding and reshaping the complex reality. And this process never ends: not only is the process itself always open-ended, but so is the result.

Thus one begins with a mythical vision, a provisional vision, of the future as an open-ended future: a future which is free to decide on *its* own future: a society in which politics can happen, in which different groups of people are able to press towards change in the society.

To get this process started, what the participatory futurist needs is a medium for the presentation of practicable desirable futures that offers human beings a chance to "work" the futures, to test them out and to invent parts of them or work out new solutions for problems that emerge from them. For the possibility of participatory futurism depends on the availability to the whole public of images of the future on which they can practice creative disorder in the present.

One way of doing this might be to cross-fertilize the simulation games used by Establishment strategists like RAND with the role-playing and highly schematic guerrilla theater used by many movement organizations to politicize their constituents or train their activists. For instance, let us imagine the creation of Future Gaming Centers—perhaps alongside radical community-organizing projects that are focused on present discontents and revulsions. Such Future Gaming Centers could offer experience in "living" alternative futures to Americans who are fed up with the present but have no feel for a workable or desirable society. They could be the first step towards broad popular involvement in the process of "creative disorder": for they would encourage the invention of model futures that could then be attempted in the present.

Such "future games" could focus on several different kinds of situations. One might project, for example, a particular sort of school system of the year 2000 in an American city: perhaps a highly automated high school whose students frequently use euphoria-creating drugs, are politically organized, and carry on political and social action with deprived groups in the community as part of training for a Peace Corps ROTC. Participants in this "game" might play the roles of parent, student, teacher, principal, city councilman, and local taxpayer, each confronted with the crisis created by the sudden advent of a powerful intelligence-enhancing drug.

Another game might pose the problem of a revolution in South Africa, in a world in which total national disarmament was being enforced by a minimal, non-governmental world police force. How would American and Soviet cabinet members, UN officials, Chinese revolutionary propagandists, and similar persons respond to the crisis and to each other's responses?

Or again, in an Indian village of the year 2000, how would the American Farm Corpsman, the Chinese revolutionary organizer, the French teacher, the Russian engineer, the Yugoslavian syndicalist labor leader, the UN development economist, the Indian government official, and the local villagers react to and upon each other?

The movement is not the only institution that could be encouraged to develop such future gaming; or, to put it another way, as the energy and appeal of the movement begins to transform particular schools, recreation centers, and private associations, these "mainstream" groups could well begin to offer alternative futures to scrutiny and testing out by their members and publics.

Nor is the neighborhood Future Gaming Center the only possible approach to participatory futurism. Public-opinion surveys that now offer people only the narrowest of choices within the present social system could be broadened to present (and vividly so that they do not seem ridiculous) possible futures or alternatives that lie outside present assumptions. The mass media might begin to show people "real" worlds that *might* be, as well as the fake world that already is, and might create new audience-feedback processes. There may be many other places in which "taking a trip" not on the latest psychedelic but on political imagination could expand the social consciousness of large numbers of people formerly imprisoned in a disastrous present.

Such efforts would require amounts of money and time that the movement does not now have available. It would also require the movement itself to shift (at least in part) from "revulsion organizing" to "attraction organizing"—a change it does not often feel emotionally able to make, under the pressure of horrors daily piled on horrors. But in the absence of such efforts, the field is almost certain to be left to the anti-democratic futurism of the present; and there can be no surer way to guarantee an undemocratic future.

16
The Campus: If You Were 20

Gentlemen, you have asked me to talk on the nature of the campus today and why there has been so much turmoil on the campus recently.* I think the best way for you to understand the American campus is to imagine yourselves out of the role of businessman, into the role of a student who is, say, 20 years old.

If you are 20 years old today, you probably first became conscious of political events when you were 15½. The great world of politics probably first intruded on your private personal life when John F. Kennedy was murdered in 1963. This had a major impact on you, partly because he was President and you had been taught all your life that the Presidency was a religious, as well as a political, institution. (Indeed, the Presidency unites the function of party leader, Prime Minister, and quasi-religious symbol, and the President is in a sense the presiding bishop of the church of democratic nationalism in the United States.) So you were deeply shocked, as were your friends and family, by the murder of the President.

But it was not just any President who was murdered. It was a President who, the media and many of the people you knew said over and over again, was the President of youth: the President who cared about you, who cared about your friends, who had the physical and sometimes the intellectual and emotional qualities of appeal to change and energy and newness in America. So you were especially deeply shocked that this particular President was killed. It shook your automatic faith in the political system and the society you had grown up in.

His successor, although he did not carry the same sense of excitement, addressed the issues that began to concern you. He

---

* This is a revised version of a talk to the Public Affairs Council, drafted the week after Robert Kennedy was murdered and given in July 1968.

spent the year after President Kennedy's death in promising to end poverty in America, to end racism and racial discrimination in America, to reduce the military budget, to achieve peace and disarmament in the world. And not only did he promise these things, but he began to act on them. You were rather pleased at his behavior and his performance. You were happy, although you could not vote, that he won more than 60% of the vote on the basis of those promises, in the election of 1964.

Perhaps a few things distressed you—you wondered why he had bothered to bomb North Vietnam in retaliation for a minor and peculiar incident in the ocean; you wondered why he had not decided to give the Mississippi Freedom Democratic Party full seating rights at the Democratic Convention; you wondered why the University of California felt it necessary to crack down so hard on students that were demanding free speech; but you were thoroughly skeptical of the tiny band of radicals who claimed that those events represented the real face of America. You confidently looked forward to the fulfillment of the promises that the President had made in order to win the election. By now you are 16½, and perhaps a few of your friends were excited about the idea of working in the civil-rights movement or were wondering whether the universities would be able to change so that people in them would not be mere items in an IBM machine. But these were probably your older friends or brothers; you were still finishing high school.

And then, in February 1965, you were stunned. The President who had promised to make peace and reduce the defense budget began to bomb North Vietnam. During the next few months, you began to realize that the professors on many leading campuses thought that the bombing was a disaster. You heard that thousands and thousands of students—again, probably including a few of your older friends—were protesting against the war. Those of your high-school friends who were not planning or not able to go on to college began to talk nervously about the draft, as the number of men drafted began to increase.

Perhaps I should go lightly over the history of the next three years of your life. It was three years during which the government you had been brought up to believe in conducted a war that you came to regard as despicable, obscene, illegal, and both

147

politically and morally stupid. But above all, obscene. Above all you found yourself sickened by every day's daily news. And it was not just the news from Vietnam. The defense budget, which the President had promised to cut, leaped from 50 billion dollars to 80 billion dollars a year. The poverty program, which the President of the United States had promised to expand, first leveled off and then began to contract. The promise that the poor would be involved in running the program was broken. You began to discover that your own campus was involved in some of the most disgusting aspects of the war—in preparing germ warfare, or in doing research on napalm.

From Black America, where you had been hoping there would be a major thrust for racial equality and full civil rights, the news got much worse. You began to hear that the Civil Rights Acts that had been passed were not being enforced. And then there began to be "riots." Everybody began talking about the violence the Negroes were using, and their attack on the traditional, peaceful, and nonviolent ways of getting social change. But then you began to look closely at the reports of the "riots." You began to realize that the deaths reported from those riots ran along the lines of 25 Black people killed, 2 whites; 38 Black people killed, 3 whites; and so on. And you began to wonder where the violence was coming from: you began to think that perhaps it was official white America, and its police, its National Guard, and its Army, that was more violent than Black communities.

But perhaps what oppressed you and distressed you worst in this whole period, was that the quasi-religious figure of the President was befouled. In a youth that had been focused by the murder of one President, and in which the Presidency had therefore taken on a special aura, the incumbent President became the index of your revulsion, not your pride. You saw the President of the United States as a liar—indeed, the media in talking about the "credibility gap" endorsed that view; as a perjurer—because he had sworn to uphold the Constitution, and was violating it by conducting a war without Congressional approval; as a murderer—because that war was illegal under international and domestic law and therefore every death of every Vietnamese and every American was not a legitimate act

148

of national defense, but instead simple murder. The President a liar, a perjurer, a murderer? How much deeper could your horror be?

But there was the promise of change, and there were men to whom you could give your respect and honor. Indeed, there were four men of national prestige whom you could begin to believe embodied your vision of what you had been taught America was supposed to be. Two of the men were American versions of secular saints and two of them were politicians. They did not always speak for the things that bothered you most, but you could see them as honorable adults; as men striving to uphold the ancient virtues in the best fashion they were able. Some of your radical friends sneered at them, but that made you uncomfortable. So you honored them. And then even here, disaster struck. Of the two secular saints, your government tried to put one of them in jail, and the other was murdered. And of the two politicians, one was murdered and the other left to walk a dusty path towards certain political defeat.

So that is your America. You are 20 years old now. Your heroes have been dishonored, killed, or attacked. Your society seems unutterably corrupt. And this process has filled the whole of your conscious political life. From the time you were 15 until now, your experience as an American has been one of betrayal.

What then ought you to believe? How then ought you to act? Do you have any reason to accept the traditional statements of law, of respect for those who hold power? Or do you have every reason to resist those who to your mind have usurped authority? Do you have any reason to respect a parliamentary, representative democracy in which the parliament has foresworn all its powers and responsibility? Or do you have every reason to grope toward some alternative form of democracy, in which parliament will be bypassed and people will be able to participate directly in controlling the institutions that control their lives?

Now suppose we step back out of the roles I asked you to take on. You and I are not 20 years old. But the world I have described is a real one, at least to them. And they have acted honorably as citizens of that world. *And they will not stop.* If you gentlemen are looking for peace and good order on the campuses, then you must address not the campuses but the leadership of your businesses and your political system. The students know it is a crime to make napalm for use in Vietnam; so they will not believe it is a crime to prevent that napalm from being made. They believe it is a crime for your companies to recruit men for research into new weapons for war; so they will not believe it is a crime to interfere with that recruitment. They believe that the drafting and even the voluntary enlistment of men into the armed services for fighting in an illegal and unconstitutional war is a crime; so they will not believe it is a crime to disrupt the draft or the enlistment offices. The turmoil that has you worried is the result of the five years of social history and personal biography that I have described to you.

I realize that many of you may say that what a 20-year-old remembers is not the history of the world. You may say that the America you remember is the real America, and the America he remembers only a brief deviation. You perhaps remember an America that stopped the Nazis, an America that assisted some underdeveloped countries to win their freedom from colonial rulers. You may remember an America in which the poor and the unemployed created a labor movement. (Even you cannot remember an America in which there was racial equality, of course.) But you will say that that is the real America, and the history of the last five years at worst a terrible mistake. (Some of you may not even believe it was a mistake; some of you may insist it was the right path. But perhaps many of you believe it was a mistake.)

But I ask you to question yourselves. Which is the real world? Is it the world that older people remember, believing that recent events are merely deviations? Or is it the world of now? Is it the world that the old remember or the world that the young live in? After all, *we* live in their world too. *That* is the world of existence, the world of reality, the world that presses in upon the life of all of us. The other is the world of nostalgia. If somehow that older, more decent America turned into this one, we must question the seeds of disaster in that older America. We cannot lightly dismiss the reality of the 20-year-old, as if it were the mere mistake of youth. Because it may indeed reflect the reality that has come to overwhelm us.

150

And in any case—*in any case*—it is the world that an entire new generation of Americans believes is real. Once there was a generation—yours—that formed itself around the event of Munich, and has been looking for Munichs ever since. Now there is a generation that will always be looking for Vietnam. It will walk into any event believing that the President is *probably* lying—that the United States is *probably* committing murder—rather than coming painfully and dreadfully to that conclusion after long torment. I think they will be the first generation of Americans who believe their government is illegitimate. And they will live for fifty years.

17

In Grant Park

[*Beginning possibly omitted.*] For two nights in a row now, from the floor, we adjourned the Convention.* And you know, hold it, you know how unusual that is. It's usually the Chair that adjourns Conventions; it's usually the Administration that adjourns Conventions; it's usually the machine that adjourns Conventions. But for two nights in a row now, by God, it's been the People that have adjourned the Convention. [*Cheers.*] We adjourned it, we adjourned it tonight, we adjourned it tonight because we thought that the votes were being stacked against us on the peace plank. And we adjourned it last night because we were damned if the Convention was going to go on that Julian Bond and the Black people of Georgia had been forced to share seats with the racists [*portion drowned out by cheers and chants of "Julian Bond, Julian Bond"*].

I want to tell you a little, I want to tell you a little about the atmosphere inside the Convention. My delegation, the District of Columbia, voted the other day to demand that the City of Chicago grant the parade permits that the Mobilization has demanded [*cheers*] and that the City of Chicago, the State of Illinois, and the President of the United States get the troops the hell out of Chicago. [*Cheers.*] I don't think any other delegation has spoken, as a delegation, but I've talked to delegate after delegate after delegate who has realized what your presence has made clear: the war is continued not only at the point of a gun in Vietnam, but at the point of a bayonet in Chicago. [*Cheers.*] In the last six months, around the world, there have been two important governments that have been toppled by nonviolent movements led chiefly by the students—the Novotny

* This speech was given on a bullhorn from the midst of the crowd in Grant Park, while delegates listened from their windows in the Conrad-Hilton Hotel, at about 2 A.M., August 28, 1968 (Tuesday night of the Democratic Convention in Chicago).

Government in Czechoslovakia and the Johnson Government in Washington. [*Cheers.*] But the Novotny Government tried to take power back at the point of a bayonet last week and the Johnson Government is trying to take power back at the point of a bayonet this week. But the people of Czechslovakia have made it hard to do. And by God the people of the United States are going to make it hard to do. [*Cheers.*]

O.K. We're going to be trying our damnedest tonight and tomorrow and, if we have to and if we can and we're ready to use the power of 5,000 on the floor of that Convention to do it, we're ready to try to prevent the re-establishment of the Johnson or the make-believe Johnson or the super-Johnson Administration at the point of a bayonet. But we're going to need your help. Whatever they tell you, we know that the cops are not protecting us from you. They are protecting Johnson from all of us. [*Cheers and chants of "Join Us, Join Us."*]

18
After Grant Park: Guerrilla Politics

The triumph of the Beatles was that avant-garde critics and the mass public joined in celebrating them—the one side dropping the pedantry of Cage, the other abandoning the silliness of Welk. Just so Chicago. Suddenly the emptiness of conventional political ideas was revealed. Suddenly avant-garde political theory and the public understanding of politics fused: Walter Cronkite, Tom Hayden, and the American Sociological Association all proclaimed—to millions at the TV screens, to thousands on the streets, to hundreds in the scholarly libraries—the advent of the police state and the death of democratic liberties.

In that fusion lay the first great political victory of the New Left since its emergence in the very early sixties. Some of the New Left movement has been successful before in transmitting some of its views to the general public—but always before these were the liberal views, the dreams of *freedom now* or *end the war*. But never before had the New Left been able to get radical departures across to the general public. Never before had the great broad liberal public been brought face to face with the thwarting of its visions and assumptions: the vision of the first amendment, the assumption that *voting works*. Chicago did that; it challenged the most important liberal dogma, the one that America is a free and democratic country with only a few major faults that need to be reformed.

For the first time, facing the failure of representative democracy inside the Convention and the use of police terror outside, millions of liberals and peaceniks caught their breath at the unthinkable: Maybe American society *as a whole* was unfree and undemocratic, and the areas of liberty mere pockets that must be defended and expanded through great struggle. For after all, Chicago was not Mississippi—a backwater to entertain and horrify—but the Second City, the heartland's capital, the keystone of the ruling Democratic Party. And this failure of electoral representative democracy was no failure in some pipsqueak city council, but a failure in the most important assembly in the land. So for the first time, millions who had disagreed on a policy issue began to connect that issue with the structure of power in America; they began to wonder whether the Government's war was against Vietnamese or against Americans; they began to doubt the legitimacy of one of the crucial political institutions. And so they became what might be called not-quite-radicals.

Not quite. And that is one measure of the limits of the New Left's victory at Chicago. For there was no program, no institution, no line of action for the new near-radicals to undertake. Three proposals are on the table: reforming the Democratic Party, building a new party, and moving into the streets. None of them has even begun to arouse the energies, hopes, and angers of the new near-radicals around the country, though small groups of leaders have struck out in one or another of these directions.

Reforming the Democratic Party appeals strongly to those who led the McCarthy/Kennedy movements and thereby gained what looks like a foothold for future power inside the party. The strength of this hope among the leaders can be seen by the horror with which even the toughest of them—like Paul O'Dwyer, senatorial candidate in New York—greeted explicit proposals for a new party or even actions that threatened to break up the old one. For example, on Wednesday night when word of the worst police brutality outside the Conrad Hilton reached the Convention floor, an emergency caucus of peace delegates voted overwhelmingly, after 15 minutes' discussion, to demand that the Convention adjourn and, if necessary, force it to do so by chanting the way they had the previous two nights ("Jul-yan BOND!" and "Let's GO HOME!"). Back on the floor, when several motions to adjourn were rejected by the Chair the temperature on the Convention floor rose to the flash point. Delegates were as ready to force an adjournment as they had been the previous night, even if it meant fighting with the Convention police. But this time, O'Dwyer, Richard Goodwin of the McCarthy staff, and other peace-caucus leaders hushed the efforts to begin a chant. Most of the peace delegates, now split up among the various states and deprived of each other's

155

militance, felt they must follow the wishes of "the leadership." Why the retreat? Because, O'Dwyer said, the Convention machine "would not permit" chanting to break up the roll call for nomination of a Presidential candidate.

What if there had been chanting anyway? The answer is clear: The party would have broken up—perhaps literally, in a thousand fistfights on the floor of the Convention. At the brink of resistance, liberal leadership stepped back—and after the session, substituted the dissent of a candlelight march.

As it is now, the grass-roots McCarthy movement is faced with great obstacles and dangers. A real reform would in effect require the expulsion of the old guard. How crucial the old guard is can be seen from the fact that from Sunday to Tuesday of the Convention, almost all the liberal delegates were looking to Richard Daley to be the savior of the party and the country. It was Daley they hoped would plump for Ted Kennedy—Daley they hoped would switch on the peace plank—Daley who held the balance of power. (What if he had done it—and on Thursday morning Ted Kennedy had faced the party as the nomineee of the Boss Cop whose men had been beating up the liberals' sons and daughters? Would they have praised their own practicality, or puked out their guts in shame?)

If the liberals were so weak that they had to look to Daley for salvation, will they be strong enough in four years' time to expel him and his kind from the party? Or will they have to settle in a four-year stretch for a candidate acceptable to the Daleys— exactly the deal they thought they wanted in Chicago? While they are trying to budge the great rock of the old guard, will their own faces turn as stony as did that of Sisyphus? (If Hubert Humphrey was ever a liberal, that is what happend to him between 1948 and 1968.) And finally, while they hurl their energies into the enormous task, will everything else stay quiet —or will the whole political structure dissolve into semi-civil war and leave them reforming in the wind? No wonder the angry peaceniks can't get excited, to such ends!

So then a new party? No—because the new near-radicals, like the delegates they sent to Chicago, have not quite mastered their own hopes for a "leader," and the leader is not available. Intrinsically, there was no reason 15 million Americans could not have decided to nominate and vote for presidential candidates who were not "national political figures." But the cry was "McCarthy!" and he wouldn't come. The stubborn few who have moved ahead are expecting that events of the next few months or years will complete radicalization of the liberals, convince them they must build their own creation without waiting for "the leaders."

But electoral politics is a numbers game, and the numbers are not yet ready for new-party politics. In their absence, many feel it makes more sense to pursue the politics of direct action, which depends on commitment rather than numbers. Could a new party of new near-radicals create hundreds of grass-roots conventions where a People's Federal Budget was worked out and put before the Congress? Can a counter-Inaugural be held that will not merely say no to the White House but present an alternative program and line of action to the baffled American people?

The streets are not enough. Simply going back to the streets may confirm the lessons of Chicago in fresh blood, but offers no new base of action and no program. In any decent rhythm of insurgent politics, it is of course important to strip the Emperor naked. Chicago not only did that, it laid bare the Emperor's leprosy. But there are moments in that rhythm when insurgents must be ready with something to wear as fresh and joyful as the miniskirt. And that moment seems to have arrived. If there is to be a real opposition (not Humphrey if Nixon wins, or Nixon if Humphrey wins), then it must create a new policy program and a new organizational form for itself.

And as the opposition grapples with this need, let it not forget the other revelation of Chicago: There is an alternative. The police riot—encouraged and abetted though it was by orders from the top, from the Center Establishment—was still a rejection of the Center. The Wallace movement (of whom the police are simply the direct-action vanguard) has deep social roots. And the Left has not so far addressed the needs of the millions of Americans who are the Wallace movement.

They are not simply racist and anti-intellectual. Almost all of them are the *working* Americans—lower-middle-class storekeepers and farmers, factory workers, secretaries—who think they are paying for other people to loaf. People on campuses—

157

who loaf on fellowships and faculty salaries, who don't really work because they enjoy what they do and control their own time. People on welfare—who loaf, period. And who pays the bill? Those who pay the property tax, the sales tax, and even— now that its progressivity has been emasculated—the income tax. Those whose wages and small-scale profits have stood still for five years, while big corporate profits have doubled. The Slow Squeeze—that is what the Wallace movement grows out of. Many of its people inveigh against Big Business and the labor bureaucrats who stifle every wildcat strike. Many of them loved Bobby Kennedy for his toughness, his streak of fury at the Establishment, his Irish gut-fighting. Some of them voted for McCarthy because he took on the Soft Machine and tried to end the war. But of course the Wallace movement directs its anger not at the enemies at the top—but at the visible non-workers, the poor and the professors.

And the Movement—the Blacks, the students, the peaceniks —have done little to address lower-middle-class anger. Who has heard of a New Left tax program, or direct action against sales or property taxes? Who has seen any student putting months of his energy into sustaining the grocery-boycott campaign against high prices that broke out in December 1966?

There are some who counsel quiet, claiming it is the Left that energizes Wallace, urging a moratorium on marches and the acceptance of the labor-leader terms for progress.

If every demand for justice invites repression, is justice achieved without demanding it? If Meany bureaucrats cannot meet the needs of the workers, shall radicals therefore hew to the Meany line?

No, the politics of immobilism cannot be the answer. Nor can blind confrontation. The lesson of Chicago is guerrilla politics —not guerrilla war. The urban guerrilla in a developed country is the man who uses his social niche and involvement as a base for action, the way Mao used Yenan—not the man who throws a rock and ducks into the alley. And, guerrilla politics requires the liberation of a new political base. Our armies of the night need new recruits. To get them we must invent a political course of action, not new street tactics.

Where are we, since Chicago? At a crossroads so breathtaking that the New Left's first great political victory could destroy it. There are two deep divisions within America. One is within the Establishment, the other within the public. There is a fight on inside the Establishment over the worth and good sense of a permanent war system. That was the meaning of the Kennedys' break with Lyndon Johnson, of the bankers' warning that an escalation of the war last February would break the dollar, of Johnson's withdrawal. The split begins with the failure of nuclear superiority to win any real victories, expands with the failure of the war, but is hammered far deeper by the growing insurgency at home and its warning that reinvestment from war to domestic reconstruction is desperately needed. If the split Establishment confronted a single broad alliance of insurgents, its problems would be enormous.

But there is no such alliance. Instead there is a confrontation that is bitterly contested. On the one side, the old classes—middle and working. On the other, the new classes—the Black or Spanish-speaking or Appalachian poor, and the university-bred. And war in the streets between their various champions.

A recipe for disaster, indeed for civil war: continued confrontation, with no program. A recipe for triumph: continued confrontation, many on new fields to engage the interest of the old classes, plus a program that allows the new near-radicals to move.

19

The Religious Upwelling on the Left

There is still a New Left—and one of the ways it shows its differences from all the old ones is by a remarkable interest in religion, magic, astrology, and the other "opiates" of traditional Left ideology.

Item: The Bread and Puppet Theater opens performances by an act of communion: the players and watchers share home-baked bread.

Item: The American Playground does a guerrilla theater raid on the White House, Easter Sunday, in which the central event is dozens of people carrying a huge, heavy cross.

Item: The movement exorcises the Pentagon.

Item: Dick Gregory chooses his Inaugural date on the basis of astrology.

Item: Thousands of radicals and peaceniks join in Freedom Seders, celebrating the Passover as a liberation holiday.

Item: Christian radicals undertake the movement's first public attack on corporate private property by scattering Dow Chemical records over downtown Washington.

Item: The resistance seeks and receives sanctuary in a number of churches.

Item: Many underground papers begin to explore mysticism and magic.

Item: Georges Pompidou remarks that after earnestly mulling over the French "May" for almost a year, he concludes it was nothing so minor as 1789 or 1917, but an earthquake in values as deep as the religious revolution of the fourth century in the Roman Empire.

Why? Of what need and demand is all this the expression? Is it a rejection of reason and intellect?

160

Let us assume that mankind is sane. Let us assume we find ourselves at the end of 250 years of "scientific" (that is rational and intellectual) effort, on the point of exterminating ourselves or—even if we avoid that catastrophe—poisoning and polluting our world. Would it be too much to expect that sane men and women would turn away from such a world, recoil from worship of the science that created it, and search for roots of prescientific thought and feeling—especially feeling—that might connect them to a sense of mankind and of nature once again? —to a sense of love, joy, and community that might color or transform the use of the technology that science made available? Is it surprising that young people begin to connect the Powers that decree war and profit from racism with the Powers that manage and advance the dehumanized technology machine?

In that context, the "religious" sense—that is, an urgency for reconnecting mind, body, and spirit—becomes not only a "morally" human response to a morally dehumanizing society, but also a "politically" liberating response to politically oppressive institutions. Naturally, in that response there might emerge some very peculiar notions of what religion should be. Indeed, the more "forbidden" a religious expression, the more scornfully it is treated by conventional society, the more attraction it might hold for the most desperate and most furious, as well as the most hopeful and loving, as a form of resistance to the conventionally celebrated death of man. Thus, perhaps, the experiments with astrology and magic.

The traditional Left analysis of the treatment of religion by those who rule the society is not wholly false, of course. The rulers encourage "freedom of religion," the "prayer breakfast," and other forms of piety that celebrate the status quo. But they are quite conscious of what forms of quasi-religious organization are in fact bureaucratized versions of the one-dimensional society, rather than perpendicular assertions of mystery, communal feeling, and some tradition that predates industrial capitalism and calls into question its omnipotence.

In California, the most secularized, one-dimensionalized, repressively desublimated province of neo-capitalism, the resistance to secularization has most fiercely erupted in religious experiment—not only in the explicit "cults," astrology, and

161

drugs, but also in such semi-religious efforts as the Esalen "encounter" movement. Freedom of religion is turned from a tolerated pluralism (where Jews, Presbyterians, Lutherans, Catholics are allowed to stay separate so long as all of them will think and act exactly like each other, "separately") into a multitude of strongly felt *different* beliefs that threaten the social peace and the social order.

In the individual biographies of those who are now experimenting/experiencing the religious impulse, the years of childhood probably determine what form it takes. For some, there were explicit religious rituals and intense communal and family feeling built around them. Then perhaps came years in high school and college during which these feelings of mystery and transcendence were buried and ignored, and the rituals rejected and scorned, in behalf of highly "rational," intellectualized, manipulable science, mathematics, and social science. Then comes the attempt to "transcend MIT" by recovering and re-translating the childhood roots into an adult fusion of intellect and mystery. Thus, Jews who were children in the 1930s and '40s may have had an especially strong exposure to specifically religious teachings, as their parents reacted to the Holocaust. For others, the true "religion" in their families may have been the celebration of the Southern Confederacy, and their adult recovery may require the reincorporation, with radical transformations, of such symbols as the Confederate flag. For still others, bereft of any such childhood experience, the call of magic and astrology may be strongest. But for many, the personal biography and the social history seem to recapitulate and strengthen each other, with the last two centuries playing for mankind as a whole the role of "the years at MIT."

Looked at from this angle, the "cultural nationalism" or "cultural revolution" that has welled up in some of the Black movements, in the Southern Student Organizing Committee, in *la huelga,* in the hippie movement, perhaps in the Women's Liberation Movement, and in some efforts at Jewish organizing may represent a real and important form of rebellion against Amerika.

This fusion of political radicalism with spiritual communion therefore seems an important direction for both The Movement (radical and typically puzzled by religion) and The Reawakening (religious and typically puzzled by radicalism) to explore. On the movement's side, there has recently been some tendency to dismiss this approach as pork-chop cultural nationalism and thus to accept "Old Left" definitions of oppression as only economic and political, throwing away some of the best insights of the "New" Left into the way the Establishment has used cultural repression to control the people and protect its highly bureaucratized system. If the movement keeps moving in this direction, it might degenerate from an allegedly revolutionary attempt to transform the country, into a mirror-image, one-dimensionalized version of the America it is trying to topple; and it might isolate itself from one of the strongest rebellious impulses welling up from the general American people —which may be discovering it is not so much a single people as all that.

The wiser response from the movement would seem to be working among "cultural revolutionaries" or the reawakened religious to lay bare the connections between cultural repression, the one-dimensional society, and political and economic exploitation on the one hand, and between cultural rebellion or nationalism and economic and political insurgency on the other. The movement should accept the fact that the system tries to expropriate our heads and hearts as well as our bodies, and also the connections among them—and should recognize the legitimacy of an effort to recover our heads and hearts for ourselves.

On the other hand, cultural rebels or religious organizers should make every effort to connect integrally the traditional or newly created religious rituals and cultural assertions with political and economic analysis (as the Jewish Organizing Project explicitly connects the Prophetic and Chassidic traditions with demands for the economic and political as well as spiritual transformation of America and the Jewish community). Worked on in these ways, the impulse for spiritual liberation need not degenerate into pie in the sky, but be closely attuned to the more usual radical demands.

There are perhaps legitimate fears that appeals to traditional rituals may inflame traditional enmities between those who

163

should be allies in revolution (as the Southern Student Organizing Committee's use of the Confederate flag, even crossed by
black-and-white handclasp, sometimes did, or as the Passover-
Easter rituals might have done). There should be no blind
obeisance to the past. The reconstruction of old rituals so that
they unite us across our separate religious senses is a task that
requires both intelligence and feeling—as does all the work
of the movement. It is no answer to say that the task is too
difficult.

20
The Lightning Flash—And After

The Vietnam War has been a lightning-bolt flung upon American society. Flung, we should note, by America's own rulers—flung against the people of Vietnam, whom our government expected to blast and melt and reshape according to its will.

But the lightning bolt boomeranged. It was caught and hurled back by the people of that tiny poverty-stricken, agrarian, fifth-rate country—because they developed revolutionary war, the fusion of politics and violence, to one of its most effective levels in all history. They were thus able to hurl the lightning back against this Super-State, this Empire with the most terrible weapons and the biggest economy and the most sophisticated universities in all world history.

When the lightning bolt landed, it had two effects: intense heat and sudden light. Every old division in American society, soldered over with great care, began to smoke and steam and melt as the heat of the lightning raised all temperatures.

• The fury of Blacks against racism reached new intensities as Blacks discovered they were called to die in battle in greatly disproportionate numbers and to postpone once again the promised abolition of their poverty—and that indeed their poverty was used to force them into the army to fight and die for the system that kept them poor.

• The anger and disengagement of the "new class" reached new intensities as they discovered their votes manipulated, their peacefulness trampled on, their educations interrupted or misdirected for utterly extrinsic reasons, their independent knowledge and information about the world, acquired at the university with such energy and pride, treated with contempt and lied about.

• Even the anger of the old working class—presumably so well integrated into the system by the New Deal with equal doses of continuously rising incomes, bureaucratic and self-limiting unions, and patriotic anti-communism—even their anger began to rise. For price inflation and high taxes caused a drop in real take-home pay and the disappearance of new housing, while war spending prevented action to save public services like schools and hospitals and telephones from collapse. And meanwhile, as the workers watched and muttered, corporation profits kept going up and Congress failed—for the first time in the twentieth century—even to impose an excess-profits tax on blood money made from war.

• Perhaps most astonishing of all, divisions inside the Establishment heated up. The 1968 "gold crisis"—in reality a dollar crisis—convinced the more sophisticated parts of the Establishment that the war was straining the American system too much, financially and politically, and that the government should cut its losses. (Thus the *Wall Street Journal,* for example.) But not all of the Establishment agreed; and the internal struggle intensified.

So as a result of the heat delivered by that lightning bolt of a war, America has indeed begun to come apart, precisely "at the seams"—at the places where our disparate parts had been soldered together. But that was not all. For the lightning bolt brought a great flash of light, too. Where before we had been stumbling around in the dark in our own society, occasionally bumping into strange objects that hurt or even killed us but that we could not see or understand, in the sudden flash of the war we were able to see the cruel engines strewn around our homes.

• We began to recognize the real purposes of "education," as we discovered that our professors were hired to invent germ warfare, our grades were submitted to Selective Service, and our choice of courses was controlled through the draft so as to channel us into "useful" rather than liberating occupations. We began to wonder why we had to create "teach-ins" at colleges and high schools in order to talk seriously about one of the great issues affecting our country—why, if "education" was supposed to lead us forth into citizenship and individuality, we were not talking about such issues all the time as part of learning. We concluded that the schools were intended to control, not liberate us.

• We discovered that the kind of democracy taught in textbooks—write your Congressman, run for office, vote in the primaries, hold public meetings—did not work. We learned that even if we *won* elections (as we did in the spring of 1968), the roads to power were blocked; that somehow the Democratic Party did not respond to the will of its electorate; that the police, the army, and the Chicago machine meant more than the will of the people. We discovered that we could even create the most widespread political event in American history (at least since the eight-hour-day general strike in 1886 or since the Civil War) as Moratorium Day in October 1969, and smack on top of that create the largest political rally in all American history, at the Mobilization in November 1969—and affect government policy not a jot. We began to realize that the civics books were wrong, and that the only actions that had brought change were such "illegal" ones as resisting the draft, raiding draft board files, confronting the Pentagon.

• We discovered that the myth that we could keep a military-espionage empire going abroad and not affect democracy at home, was false—as witness the CIA's corruption of some student, labor, and religious organizations.

• We realized that our military professionals were either idiots or liars. Their repeated predictions of victory in Vietnam, their bafflement in the face of revolutionary warfare, taught us to look more closely at their everyday proposals. So we discovered that the ABM and MIRV were crazy; not that the rest of the arms race since 1945 had been sane, but we had never looked before.

• We discovered—most frightening of all—that our rulers are not even capable of ruling in what their smartest people know, and we can recognize, is *their own* best interests. Thus they have proved unable to end the war even though it is clearly in their interest to get it ended. Perhaps, indeed, they are in that most dangerous position for an Establishment: unable to reform itself. For what they clearly need to do is to abolish the war system, to release the money and emotion and energy now tied up in it in order to soothe and pay off domestic insurgencies. But they may be unable to end the war system if that requires abolishing an $80-billion-a-year institution which commands one-tenth of the national economy. Who ever heard of abolishing such an institution without a great social upheaval? We would have to think of cases like Henry VIII's expropriation of the monasteries—but Henry VIII had an army to do it with. If the American Establishment cannot survive if the war system continues, but cannot act to end it, then where are we?

From all these discoveries, we now know things about America that are *not new* because of the war, but were lit up to our gaze by the war. Our education, our politics, our military had been incompetent, inhuman, and undemocratic—as we now can see—before Lyndon Johnson escalated the war in 1965. But most of us had never tried seriously to confront the civics books before; and so we didn't know.

Once the old myths were stripped away, we began discovering some things that were even more important about our country. We learned that our rulers make war not only upon the Vietnamese, not only upon the Blacks, but upon "us" too: upon whites with solid incomes and regular jobs, and upon "our" children. For once the myths of democracy, humanity, and competence were stripped from the Establishment, we discovered that General Motors—which for all our lives has been telling us that we kill ourselves and each other in their automobiles by falling asleep, getting drunk, and making mistakes—we discovered that GM has been killing us. Making war on us. Giving us—no, not giving us, of course; *selling* us; that is the point—cars that were *bound* to kill us. I think it is important that we discovered this only after Vietnam lit up the scene for us, let us learn that those who rule us don't mind murdering Vietnamese babies. So why should they mind killing ours?

It is not only the automobiles, of course. It is the Black Lung they impose on mine workers—because it is more profitable not to bother preventing it. It is the air and water pollution they impose on all of us—because it is more profitable not to bother preventing it. It is the abominable medical care they impose on us—because good hospitals, neighborhood health centers, and medical schools would take money out of their pockets. If we die for the sake of their profit and power, are we not war victims? And if so, what should we do about it?

In deciding what to do, we should try to draw on the experience of those two remarkable political events, the October Moratorium and the November Mobilization. Of the two, the Moratorium talked a much more limited politics—but was in process much more radical. For the Moratorium *required*— though it never said so—that people take matters into their own hands, rather than depend on a few leaders of the movement or a few rulers of the country. To stop "business as usual" on a work day; to demand time and space for anti-war teach-ins, rallies, vigils from employers, schools, and churches that were reluctant to give it; to organize thousands of independent actions—all of this required the emergence of a gutsy grass-roots leadership. The massing of 500,000 or more people at the Washington Monument on a Saturday required perhaps much more energy from a few people, but much less from a large number.

And what is even more important, the grass-roots, working-day focus of October had stunning implications for transforming the country without the "permission" of the government. For it is in Detroit, Stamford, Fort Dix, and Madison that America keeps running. It is in factories and offices and military camps that "power" is created—though it is in Washington and New York that power is collected and channeled. When 500,000 people showed up in Washington, they were petitioning an all-powerful government to change its policies. When millions rallied on a working day, they were interrupting the creation of power at its source, and were showing that they could hold power themselves.

But even that was not enough, of course. For it was still chiefly the new class that interrupted its work and confronted its own home institutions. The old working class must join in an alliance with the new and under classes if change is to be made. So the "peace movement," which is mostly a new-class affair, must reach out to the workers and identify the issues like taxes and prices and profits on which the war has affected

169

working-class life. It must identify the Death Machine that kills Americans without ever firing a bullet or dropping napalm with the War Machine that kills Vietnamese: they are ultimately the same machine. It must be ready to resist those parts of the Death Machine that workers are increasingly recognizing and opposing in exchange for the support of workers against the War Machine. It must be willing not merely to chant "End the War," but to ask who pays for the war—in high taxes, in frozen wages, in high prices, in unattainable mortgage money, in miserable public services. It must discover who profits from the war, and to block their activities with as much vigor as it brings to bear against the draft. It must be prepared to transcend its old forms of organization by neighborhoods or church or political club, and organize according to workplace; to keep involved as citizens from 8 to 11 P.M., but add a new involvement as citizens from 9 A.M. to 5 P.M. by circulating political newsletters on the job, holding lunchtime meetings to discuss political issues, demanding space to hear a speaker in the afternoon, requesting reports from management as to the war work and the tax payments of their company, planning for conversion of their work to peaceful purposes.

That transformation will not be easy, though such groups as —of all people!—Federal employees are beginning to manage it. But it must be done. The greatest hope that I see in the movement is the fact that the New Mobilization Committee has begun to try to make that shift, and is trying to make the spring of 1970 a springboard into the *new* new politics of the '70s.

Success would require two great changes. The workers would have to identify their own deprivation, discover that it is possible to organize enough power to do something about them, and get over their hang-up about people who "don't work"— whether on the campus or in the ghetto. The "non-workers" would have to get over their snobbery about hard-working people, would have to discover the deprivations they share (such as pollution) with workers, and decide to do something real about them, instead of tamely meeting in the evening and demonstrating on Saturdays. If we can both succeed, we can transform American society, with or without the agreement of its present governors.

But if we fail, Chicago in August of 1968 will become a kind of Bleeding Kansas: the model for a new form of civil war. On the one hand the old classes of the factory, the office, and the grocery store; on the other the new classes of the campus and the ghetto. Yippies and Black youth as the shock troops of one side, policemen as shock troops for the other. Not "the revolution" of so many fears and dreams, but a bloody and exhausting and paralyzing civil war.

If we fail, we lose not only the chance for a democratic, free, and communitarian America. We lose the chance to prevent the poisoning of our planet; we lose the chance to liberate the hungry nations of the Southern hemisphere; we lose the chance to prevent the nuclear destruction of the Northern hemisphere. We lose, in short, the chance to crack the Super-powers that are the most dangerous institutions in human history.

An Agenda: That Is, FOR ACTION

If we are to move ahead in the 1970s to build a democratic America, we need to learn from our experience—especially, in a sense, from what we have not even tried. I would propose some basic guidelines to be applied to some new issues and arenas:

Every action should include an element of actually learning how to run an institution or a process in a democratic way: an institution or process that creates or collects real power in the society, such as a bank, a newspaper, a factory, living quarters. In that sense each action should try to build a model of a piece of the decent society. For more people will rally to the defense of a decent institution whenever the old Establishment tries to smash it than will support a simple-minded confrontation that is not built around the seeds of an alternative, but only around anger. Moreover, we will ourselves learn how to keep things going in a free society—a knowledge which is necessary if we are not simply to surrender power to some new elite after a social convulsion.

Most actions should stretch across class lines, and try to focus on issues that unite the new and under classes with the old working and lower-middle classes on behalf of democratization of America. This does not mean that a movement from one class should abandon such issues as opposition to the Vietnam War because the established movements of another class (for example the AFL-CIO) are hostile; it does mean raising "difficult" issues in such a way as to reach out to involve others at the base, as the GI movement has reached out to young men from all classes to resist death and oppression in the Army. We have built our initial "base" in the new class and under-class; it is time to move out. Politics has a rhythm: We must learn to alternate organizing within one group around "its own" issue with seeking out the issues deeply felt by that group that are

172

also deeply felt by others. All the following issues and arenas stretch across class lines:

1. *Ecology/technology.* This must be seen in ways that go totally beyond the Nixon/Corporate anti-pollution reform measures. Those, indeed, will not work—only shift the site of pollution—so long as the present technology and its Big-Corporate bias are left undisturbed. Moreover, the high pollution industries are those that are most energy-intensive, and have a low human input. Atomic energy pollutes; good schools don't. The high-energy industries are now heavily military, and protecting the environment is closely related to abolishing war. Thus Nixon's promise to end pollution will come back to bite him in the ass as harshly as Lyndon Johnson's promise to end poverty did: more, because it was promised to many more people and its failure will anger many more. We must be creating the kind of technology that will serve decentralized groups, that does not require huge factories and the spilling of great heaps of matter and energy—heat and radiation as well as garbage and gas—into the air and water. We should be looking hard at workplace pollution: the air inside the factory is often much worse than what is spilled outside. Project: creation of a village/technology-research-institute/factory that is small, democratically controlled, and focused on inventing and applying a new small-scale but high-payoff technology that does not pollute.

2. *Celebration/liberation.* Reunification of insurgent politics and ecstatic religion, in such ways as to resist the state and its idolatry. Especially important: the creation or revivification of religious movements that stretch across national boundaries, and both mobilize transnational loyalties and provide material assistance for those who resist. Project: an International Catholic Underground made up of small, communitarian congregations in close touch with each other in Holland, America, France, Italy, Brazil, the Philippines—offering asylum to the Berrigans, carrying on political demonstrations against Brazilian torture, creating new liturgies for such universal Holy Days as Hiroshima Day.

173

3. *Worker-community control.* Both in new "businesses" like the underground press and communitarian farms and in older schools, shops, and industries, the creation of workers councils that arrange with the people of the surrounding community how to make work conditions human, how to make sure the product serves people instead of killing them (like automobiles), etc. *Not* the "nationalization of the means of production," but something much closer to "neighborhoodization."

4. *Family liberation.* The present woman's liberation movement should in effect be joined by men so that together people can seek out ways of democratizing relations between men and women, children and adults. The family may have to expand again, this time not along the lines of "blood" relationship but in communities of interest and enjoyment. Probably only this way can women and men both be liberated to make child-rearing a joy instead of drudgery and the other kinds of productive labor a serious, unalienated pursuit—instead of a mystery (as now for most women) or a bore (as now for most men).

5. *Health.* For the arenas of sickness and death to be removed from the control of the people means that their whole lives are. Projects: neighborhood-based health centers-medical schools under the control of people chosen by the patients and the neighborhood, in which the physicians are committed to teach medical practice to everyone in the community, and to admit them to whatever level of practice their competence allows, meanwhile shaping their medical practice and research in the directions the community desires.

And so on. Build the new society within the shell of the old!